Institute of Health and Social Care Research
Mental Health Research Group

TITLE OF PROJECT
Ecstasy Use in Devon & Cornwall

START DATE OF PROJECT
01/02/02

END DATE OF PROJECT
31/01/03

PERIOD OF THE REPORT
01/02/02 – 07/02/03

RESEARCHERS ENGAGED ON THE PROJECT
Project Director: Keith Lloyd
Lead researcher: Christine Brown
Research Assistant: Tobit Emmens

PUBLISHED BY
The Mental Health Research Group, Peninsula Medical School

CONTENTS

EXECUTIVE SUMMARY	3
1 – INTRODUCTION	4
2 – BACKGROUND & LITERATURE REVIEW	4
What do we know already	4
How much ecstasy is seized by the authorities?	4
How many people take ecstasy?	5
Who takes ecstasy?	8
How much ecstasy do they take?	9
What other drugs are taken by ecstasy users?	11
3 – METHODS	12
Who is included in this study?	12
What exactly did we do?	12
4 – SURVEY RESULTS	14
Who responded to the survey?	14
Taking ecstasy	16
What other drugs had respondants taken?	22
5 – QUALITATIVE DATA	24
"Good times"	24
"Bad times"	26
"E experts"	27
"E careers"	29
"E v. the rest"	31
6 – DISCUSSION	32
What are the strengths and limitations of this study?	32
What new information does this study add?	32
7 – CONCLUSIONS	34
8 – RECOMMENDATIONS	34
REFERENCES	35
APPENDIX A	37
APPENDIX B	37
Notes	38

EXECUTIVE SUMMARY

What is this study?

The study is titled: Ecstasy Use in Devon & Cornwall. The primary aim is to find out how people living in Devon and Cornwall are currently using the drug "ecstasy" (MDMA).

Who has done this research?

The research has been conducted by the Mental Health Research Group, part of the Institute of Health and Social Care, Peninsula Medical School, in collaboration with the Devon Partnership NHS Trust. The Project Director was Dr. Keith Lloyd, Senior Lecturer in Mental Health, Peninsula Medical School and Research & Development Director, Devon Partnership NHS Trust. The project team were Christine Brown, Specialist Registrar in Addictions, Devon Partnership NHS Trust and Tobit Emmens, Research Assistant, Peninsula Medical School and Research and Development Administrator, Devon Partnership NHS Trust. The project was guided by a Steering Committee made up of key participants from Health Service, University, Constabulary and Non-Statutory Agencies across the region (see appendix A for Steering Group members). The study was funded through Section 27 of the Misuse of Drugs Act 1971.

Why was it done?

There is little research evidence into patterns of ecstasy use – who takes ecstasy, how often, how much and with what else. There have been few studies asking ecstasy users their views on the risks of taking ecstasy. This is a problem for all agencies involved with drug users: health service providers are uncertain how to plan effective services for users, the criminal justice system has little expert evidence to advise in legal proceedings, and non-statutory agencies lack good quality information to advise clients. Research is needed to inform the decision-making process.

Summary of findings

A total of 411 people from across Devon and Cornwall returned anonymous questionnaires. Over three-quarters of respondents used ecstasy at least once a month on a regular basis. Nearly 85% of respondents had used ecstasy within the last month. All had used ecstasy within the last 12 months.

Respondents told us that on the last occasion they had used the drug they had consumed an average of 3 to 3.5 (95% CI = 3.04-3.52) ecstasy pills in a 24-hour period. Over the most recent weekend of ecstasy use respondents had taken on average 4 to 6 ecstasy pills (95%CI = 4.69-5.57). In case the last time respondents had used ecstasy was unrepresentative we also asked people to estimate their typical habit. Respondents said that their typical 24-hour ecstasy consumption was between 4 to 5 tablets (95%CI=4.20-4.88) and their maximum 24-hour consumption was 7 to 8 ecstasy pills (95%CI = 7.39-8.42).

Many respondents took other street drugs at the same time that they consumed ecstasy. 207 respondents (or 50.4% of the sample) took amphetamines with their ecstasy and 200 (48.7%) took cocaine with their ecstasy. 79 (19.2%) reported using cocaine when coming down from ecstasy. 19 (4.6%) reported using opiates when coming down from ecstasy.

When they were not using ecstasy many respondents reported using other street drugs. 205 (49.9%) took cocaine at times when they were not using ecstasy. 171 (41.6%) took amphetamine at times when they were not using ecstasy.

Overall 335 (81.5%) of respondents took other street drugs (not counting alcohol or cannabis) either with ecstasy or at other times. In other words more than 8 out of 10 ecstasy users responding to this survey were class A poly-substance abusers.

What will happen to the results?

The full report is available to all interested parties via the Mental Health Research Group. Copies of the executive summary can be downloaded from **http://www.ex.ac.uk/dmh**. Key findings will be presented to local stakeholders in a variety of ways.

A version of this study will be submitted for publication in the peer reviewed scientific literature and presented at international scientific meetings.

1 – INTRODUCTION

This is the final report and findings of the Ecstasy Use in Devon and Cornwall research project undertaken by the Mental Health Research Group, Peninsula Medical School in collaboration with Devon Partnership NHS Trust.

Aims

The aims of this study were:
- To determine patterns of use of ecstasy in Devon & Cornwall
- To investigate user's attitudes and risk perception of ecstasy use.

Policy relevance: national

At the national level, there have recently been calls that ecstasy should be regraded, from a class A drug to class B (Select Committee on Home Affairs. Third Report, 2002). However, there have also been 81 deaths related to taking ecstasy in England and Wales between 1997-2000 (Schifano et al 2003). In view of this debate, it is important to have a greater understanding of the use of ecstasy in the context of specific communities in Britain in order to assess the impact of any proposed policy changes.

Policy relevance: local

At the local level, the number of new cases of persons registering with a drug misuse problem using ecstasy or cocaine rose over the five-year period 1996-2001, with 2% (n=390) registering with a primary ecstasy problem and 5.8% (1090) with a secondary ecstasy problem (Wilkinson et al, 2002). There have also been deaths related to ecstasy use in the South West region. Good quality information on local patterns of ecstasy use will aid regional service planning and inter-agency working across the South West.

2 – BACKGROUND & LITERATURE REVIEW

What do we know already?

To make best use of what is already known about ecstasy use, a systematic review of published research was completed. This was done using electronic journal databases (MEDLINE, EMBASE, PSYCHLIT), government statistics (Home Office Research Development Statistics, the Office of National Statistics) and supplemented with hand searches of key journals (Addiction, International Journal of Drug Policy).

Articles that were about the neurochemical effects of ecstasy in animals or humans were not included in the review. These articles did not contain information about how ecstasy was used by people outside experimental conditions. We did include articles that had information about how many people take ecstasy, what sort of people take ecstasy, how much ecstasy they take and what other drugs are taken with ecstasy.

What is ecstasy?

Ecstasy (MDMA) is a synthetic drug, that is, it does not occur naturally but has to be chemically synthesised in a laboratory. It was adapted from methamphetamine in 1914 by Merck laboratories. The chemical name of ecstasy is 3,4 methylendioxi-metamphetamine, often abbreviated to MDMA. It became popular on the west coast of America in the 1970s when it was used as an adjunct to psychological therapy (Shulgin 1995). It was banned in 1985 because of increasing recreational use.

What is the current legal status of ecstasy in the UK?

The Misuse of Drugs Act (1971) classifies ecstasy under class A. This is the same category as heroin, cocaine and LSD. The maximum penalty for possession is a seven-year prison sentence and a fine. The maximum penalty for trafficking is life imprisonment and a fine.

How much ecstasy is seized by the authorities?

Nationally
In the UK in 2000, the number of seizures of ecstasy-type drugs was 9 670 (Corkery 2002). This consisted of 6.5 million doses of ecstasy, mostly seized by police but also by HM Customs & Excise. Ecstasy-type drugs made up 8% of the total of illegal drugs impounded. The number of ecstasy seizures has risen by 46% since 1999 and the quantity of ecstasy seized

has risen by 3% since 1999. In 25% of police forces, ecstasy is the most frequently seized class A drug. The principle source of ecstasy seized in the UK is the Netherlands, Belgium, France and Spain. The value of the total amount of ecstasy seized at street prices in 2000 was estimated at £58 813 000.

Locally
The quantity of ecstasy seized by Devon & Cornwall police in 2000 was 14 475 doses (Corkery 2002). This was 1.9% of the total quantity seized in the UK. The street price of ecstasy in Exeter and Plymouth in December 2000 was estimated at £5 per dose (Corkery 2002). This compares with a UK average of £9 per dose.

How many people take ecstasy?

International Surveys
In 2002, the Annual Report on Substance Misuse in the European Union estimated that 0.5 – 5% of the adult population had tried ecstasy (EMCDDA, 2002). This figure was based on a meta-analysis of national general population surveys on drug use conducted in eleven European countries. This study also found 10 – 30% of adults had tried cannabis, and 1 – 5% had tried cocaine. Other general population survey in Germany and Italy produced similar results, with 4 – 6.6% of the population having tried ecstasy.

The National Household Survey on Drug Abuse in the USA, 2001 found that 3.6% of people aged 12 years or more had tried ecstasy. This study also found that 5.4% of people aged 12 years or more had tried cannabis and 0.7% had tried cocaine.

Table 1: International general population surveys on prevalence of ecstasy use

EMCDDA 2002	11 EU member states, 2002		National surveys on drug misuse	0.5-5% of adults had tried ecstasy in their lifetime, compared with 10-30% cannabis, 1 –5% cocaine.
Leib et al (2002)	Germany, 1995-1999	N= 3021 base-line, 2462 at 2 year follow-up, aged 14-24 years at base-line,	Random sample from population registry	6.6% reported lifetime ecstasy use. Of those who had used ecstasy or amphetamine, 53% had an alcohol use disorder. Ecstasy users had higher rates of mental disorders compared with non-users and other illicit users, BUT their first use of ecstasy was after the onset of mental disorder in majority of cases.
National Household Survey on Drug Abuse,	USA 2001	N= 68 929, aged 12 years and above	Private households	3.6% had tried ecstasy in their lifetime, compared with 5.4% cannabis, cocaine 0.7%
Schuster et al (1998)	Germany, 1990 - 1995	n= 3 021, 14-24 yrs	community sample	4% male 2.3% female lifetime ecstasy use, 2 x increase from a 1990 survey.
Siliquini et al (2001)	Piedmont, Italy, 1998	n=3274, 18 years	Random sample of military conscripts having medical examination	4.6% lifetime ecstasy use

UK surveys

The British Crime Survey 2002 (Aust et al. 2002) found that 2.2% of 16-59 year olds and 6.8% of 16-24 year olds across England and Wales had used ecstasy in the last year. This was compared with 26.9% who had used cannabis, 5% who had used amphetamines, 4.9% who had used cocaine, 1.2% who had used LSD and 0.3% who had used heroin. The average (mean) age of first ecstasy use was 17.2 years. The estimated number of ecstasy users aged 16-59 years old in England and Wales was 680 000, 384 000 of which were aged 16-24 years old (Aust et al 2002). Using the 2001 Census data (ONS 2003), the population of 15-24 year olds in Devon and Cornwall (including the Isles of Scilly) was 127 903. This gives an estimated number of ecstasy users aged 15-59 years old in Devon and Cornwall of 14 989, 8 697 of which are aged between 15-24 years old.

4% of 16-59 year olds reported having tried ecstasy at least once in their lifetime (Coulthard et al 2002), compared with 24% who had tried cannabis, 7% amphetamines, 4% cocaine and less than 1% heroin. A meta-analysis of British Crime surveys from 1993-1996 shows an increase in ecstasy use by 16-24 year olds of one third during this time (Gore et al 1999). A sample of university students aged 18-65 years found that 13% had used ecstasy in their lifetime, compared with 57% who had used cannabis, 19% amphetamines, 5.4% cocaine and 3.2% opiates (Webb et al 1996).

Table 2: National general population surveys on prevalence of ecstasy use

Aust et al (2002)	British Crime Survey, UK, 2001-2002	N = 32 797, 16-59yrs	Random stratified sample of private households in England & Wales.	2.2% 16-59yr olds used ecstasy in the last year, 6.8% 16-24yr olds used ecstasy in the last year
Coulthard et al (2002)	UK, 2000	N= 8 580, 16-74 yrs	Stratified random sample of private households in UK	4% of 16 – 74 yr olds had used ecstasy in their lifetime, compared with 24% cannabis, 7% amphetamines, 4% cocaine, 4% LSD, and less than 1% heroin.
Gore et al (1999)	UK, 1993-1996	Meta analysis	British Crime Survey 1994-96, HEA (NCDS) 1995-96, HEMS 1996	Reported use of ecstasy by 16-24yr olds 4.8% in 1993-95 and 7% in 1996. This is an increase in ecstasy use by one third during the mid-1990s.
Ramsey et al (2001)	UK, 2000	British Crime Survey 2000, n= 13 021, 16-59yrs	Stratified random sample of private households	5% of 16-59yrs had used ecstasy, 12% of16-29yrs.
Webb et al (1996)	UK	N=3075, 18-65yrs	10 UK universities, stratified sample for sex, age and faculty, given questionnaire at beginning of class	13% had used ecstasy compared with 57% cannabis, 19% amphetamine, 18% LSD, 5.4% cocaine, 3.2% opiates

School Surveys

A review of published literature on drug use in school age children (13-17 years) from 36 countries found that rates of reported ecstasy use were highest in the UK at 6-12% and Ireland at 9% (Smart & Ogbourne 2000). A recent UK national schools survey of 10-15 year olds showed that ecstasy use began in 12-13 year old males at a rate of 1% but that by the age of 14-15 years a greater proportion of females (3%) than males (2%) reported ecstasy use (Balding 2001). 17% of 11-15 year olds reported having been offered a stimulant, which included both ecstasy and cocaine (Boreham & Shaw 2001). The USA Monitoring the Future study showed a recent decrease in the number of 17-18 year olds reporting taking ecstasy, from 9.2% in 2001 to 7.4% in 2002 (Johnston et al, 2002).

Table 3: School surveys on prevalence of ecstasy use

Balding (2001)	UK, 2000	N= 42073 10-15 yrs	Survey of participant schools, non-random sample	1% of 12-13 year old males had taken ecstasy, (0 females), 2% of males and 3% of females aged 14-15 yrs took ecstasy
Boreham & Shaw (2001)	England 2000	N= 7089, 11-15yrs	Random school and pupil sample	17% said they had been offered a "stimulant" which includes cocaine & ecstasy.
Forsyth & Barnard (1999)	Scotland, 1997	N= 2558, 14-15 year olds	Schools in rural and urban areas	4.4% of 14-15 year olds had taken ecstasy. There was no significant difference in ecstasy use between urban and rural schools.
Forsyth et al (1997)	Scotland, 1996	N= 1523, 12-15 year olds	Schools in rural and urban areas	3.1% of 12-15 year olds had taken ecstasy. There was a significant association with ecstasy use and a preference for rave music.
Johnston et al (2002)	USA, 2002	N= 43700 aged 17-18 years	School survey	7.4% high school seniors reported taking ecstasy in the last year compared with 9.2% in 2001.
Lynskey et al (1999)	Australia 1996	N= 29 447, 12-17 yrs	Secondary school students	4.4% of males and 2.9% females had taken ecstasy, the highest rate of use was 16 year old males and 17 year old females
Pedersen & Skrondal (1999)	Norway, 1996	n= 10 812, 14-17 yr olds	Total cohort of adolescents enrolled at school in capital city	3% had used ecstasy over the last year, 12.9% cannabis, 2.8% amphetamines, 1.5% heroin. Ratio of male::female ecstasy use was 2::1. Of those who had used ecstasy, 65.8% also used cannabis, 56% amphetamines, 31.5% heroin. Ecstasy use was associated with polydrug use and music subculture & house parties.
Smart & Ogborne (2000)	International 1990-1999, 36 countries (26 European)	Aged 13-17 years	Published articles on drug use in school age children	Ecstasy use was highest in UK (12- 6%) & Ireland 9%, Netherlands 5%, Belgium 5%, Italy 4%. Most Eastern European countries reported no ecstasy use in children.
Wright & Pearl (2000)	UK 1969-1999	N= 274 14-15yrs in 1999	All pupils in year 10 present on survey day from 3 schools.	Reports of knowing someone who took ecstasy began in 1989 at 2 %, in 1994 13%, in 1999 11%; reported offered ecstasy in 1994 16%, in 1999 9%.

Who takes ecstasy?

Certain groups of people have a higher rate of ecstasy use than the general public. We have already seen that the age group 16-24 years has a higher rate of use compared with other age groups (Aust et al 2002). Another association is with dance music and events, typically large informal gatherings in the mid to late 1990s known as raves. Rates of ecstasy use in rave attendees have been reported as 75-91% (Forsyth 1996, Lenton et al 1997, Riley et al 2001), in nightclub goers 81-89% (Arria et al 2002, Conner & Sherlock 1998). 52% of gay and bisexual male nightclub goers have reported using ecstasy within the last year (Klitzman 2000). Certain holiday destinations have been reported to have a higher rate of ecstasy use in UK based holiday makers (Bellis et al 2000). In a sample of opiate users attending treatment services, 90% had used ecstasy in their lifetime. Studies comparing reported ecstasy use with actual ecstasy use as identified by bioassay on urine or saliva samples showed that nearly all people who reported taking ecstasy had taken ecstasy (Arria et al 2002, Brown et al 1995).

Table 4: Selected population surveys on ecstasy use

Arria et al (2002)	USA, 2000	N= 96, 18 yrs +	Rave attendees leaving 5 nightclubs	89% had used ecstasy in lifetime, 18% reported using ecstasy last 48hrs, 20% tested positive for ecstasy on saliva sample.
Bellis et al (2000)	Ibiza, 1999	n=846, 15 - 35 years	respondents in airport departure queues returning to UK	32% had used ecstasy either in UK or Ibiza; More people had used ecstasy in Ibiza only. Boys et al (1997)
Boys et al (1997)	Australia, 1995	n=83, 13-48 years	respondents to fliers/radio programme & snowball sample on raves	31% of respondents used ecstasy in association with attending a rave event.
Brown et al (1995)	Edinburgh, UK	N= 25 16-25 yrs	Rave attenders reporting drug use	21 out of 25 reported ecstasy use, 17 confirmed MDMA or MDEA by urine sample, 4 ephedrine/pseudoephedrine only.
Conner & Sherlock (1998)	UK	N= 203, 18 -38 years	Mailing list of nightclubs	81% of nightclub attenders reported lifetime ecstasy use.
Forsyth (1996)	Glasgow UK, 1993-94	N= 135, 14-44 year olds	Snowball sample recruited by dance drug workers	91% of attendees at rave events reported lifetime ecstasy use.
Gervin et al (2001)	Ireland, 1998	N= 102, 15-31 years	Opiate users presenting to secondary services	90% of opiate users had used ecstasy in their lifetime. 67% had used opiates to come down from ecstasy; 27% reported this as their main experience with opiates.
Klitzman et al (2000)	New York	N= 169	Gay/bisexual men going into nightclubs	52% had used ecstasy in the last year compared with 92% alcohol, 60% cannabis, 38% ketamine, 32% cocaine, 25% hallucinogens, 22% inhaled nitrates, 20% amphet. Ecstasy use was significantly associated with unprotected anal intercourse.
Lenton et al (1997)	Perth, Australia, 1995	n=83, 13 - 48 years	Rave attenders who responded to advert in newspaper, fliers in shops, radio publicity	75.9% had used ecstasy in their lifetime compared with 98.8% alcohol, 96.4% cannabis, 90.4% LSD, 83.1% inhalants, 68.7% amphets, 19.3% cocaine, 12% ketamine, 7.2% heroin.
Pavis & Cunningham (1999)	Scotland 1996	70 hrs participant observation of 15-16 year olds	Youth outreach worker on Friday & Saturday nights 7pm- 3am in informal unstructured settings	Under 16 yr olds hanging out on street corners in a small scottish town took alcohol, cannabis, amphetamine, LSD & ecstasy.

Riley et al (2001)	Edinburgh, Scotland, 1998-1999	n=122, 16-47 years	dance event attendees who approached drug info stand & volunteered to fill in form	82% used ecstasy, 81.1% amphetamines, 48.4% cannabis, 38.5% cocaine, 30.3% LSD, 19.7% nitrites, 12.3% ketamine, 4.9% crack, 2.5% 2CB, one methadone user no heroin users.
Sherlock & Conner (1999)	UK, 1996	n=4042 e users, 15 - 51 years	respondents to questionnaire published in national dance magazine, circulation 80 000	80.7% current ecstasy users compared with lifetime cannabis use 95.4%, amphetamines 95.5%, LSD 74.1%, cocaine 59.3%, heroin 14.8%, crack 14.1%. Less than 0.5% had only ever used ecstasy
Tossman et al (2001)	Europe 1998 (based in 7 capital cities)	n=3503, 12 - 49 years (500 from each country)	Techno party attendees agreeing to be interviewed.	Ecstasy use varied from 83.4% in Amsterdam to 30.5% in Rome. In all cities, the rate of cannabis use was over 80%. Amphetamine use varied from 61.3% in Amsterdam to 21.3% in Rome. Cocaine use varied from 68.3% in Madrid to 21.3% in Prague.
Williams et al (1998)	London, UK 1995-1996	32 440 A&E attendances aged 15-30 yrs	Computer records for A&E attendance one hospital	48 cases of ecstasy related problems.
Winstock et al (2001)	UK, 1999	n=1151, no published age	respondents to dance magazine survey, circulation 50 000, rr = 2.3%	96% lifetime ecstasy users compared with 92% amphetamine, 91% cannabis, 77% amyl, 75% cocaine, 71% LSD, 31% benzodiazepines, 26% Ketamine, 13% GHB, 12% heroin, 5% 2CB.

How much ecstasy do they take?

Different methods have been used by different researchers to describe the average number of ecstasy pills taken. The arithmetical mean is the sum of all reported values divided by the number of participants, the median is the middle value of all those reported and the mode is the most frequent value. Other studies have reported values as a range of figures. Maximum ecstasy use on one occasion is reported as much higher than average use, though as time scales for reporting maximum use vary, for example over 24hours or over a weekend, it is difficult to compare reported values.

On examining all the studies presented in table 5 we can say that the mean numbers of pills taken on an average occasion ranged between 1 and 4. The overall range of the number of pills used on an average occasion was 0.5 – 8. The overall mean number of pills ever taken on one occasion ranged between 2 and 9. The overall range of the maximum number of pills ever taken on one occasion was 0.5 – 30.

Table 5: Reported ecstasy consumption

Boys et al (1999)	London, UK	n=100, 16-24 years	snowball sample of ecstasy users recruited by waitress, students and drug dealer	22% had used ecstasy in last 90 days, average number of pills consumed (mean) 1.6, range 0.5 – 6.
Boys et al (2001)	UK, 1998	N= 364, 16-22 years	Snowball sample of polysubstance users	Of 177 ecstasy users, average number of pills used on one occasion (mean) 1.7, range 0.5 – 5.

Study	Location	Sample	Recruitment	Findings
Calafat et al (1998)	France, Italy, Netherlands, Portugal & Spain	N= 1 627, 18 – 59 yr olds.	E users + matched controls (non-e users) group 1: disco attenders, group 2: university students recruited by snowball sample	Average number of pills used on one occasion in all 5 cities (mode) 1, (mean) 1.5. 6.2% of the overall sample used 3-4 pills on a usual occasion and only 3.4% of the overall sample reported taking 4 or more pills on a usual occasion.
Conner & Sherlock (1998)	UK	N= 203, 18 -38 years	Mailing list of nightclub goers	Average number of pills used on one occasion (median) 1.5 range 0.5 – 7.
Forsyth (1996)	Glasgow UK, 1993-94	N= 135, 14-44 year olds	Snowball sample recruited by dance drug workers	Average number of pills used on previous occasion (mean) 1.2 pills.
Handy et al (1998)	Cardiff, 1994-1995	N= 389	Clubgoers and ravers distributed by drugs outreach worker	Average number of pills used on one occasion (mean) 1.7 pills, range 0.5-8 pills. Maximum numbers of pills ever used over a weekend (mean) 3.2 pills, range 0.5-30 .
Hansen et al (2001)	Perth, Australia, 1998-2000	n= 31, 18-41 years	respondents to adverts who had used e in last 6/12	Average number of pills used on one occasion 0.5-1.5 pills.
Riley et al (2001)	Edinburgh, Scotland, 1998-1999	n= 122, 16 -47 years	dance event attendees who approached drug info stand & volunteered to fill in form	Average number of pills used on one occasion (mean) 4.18 pills. 35.2% used ecstasy weekly, 5.7% more than weekly, 19.7% once a month.
Schifano et al (1998)	Padova, Italy, 1991 - 1996	n= 150	Attendees at addiction treatment unit who reported ecstasy use	50% of ecstasy users took 1 pill only when using, maximum reported use on one occasion (mean) 3 pills, range 1.25-5
Sherlock & Conner (1999)	UK, 1996	n= 4042 e users, 15 - 51 years	respondents to questionnaire published in national dance magazine, circ 80 000	Average number of pills used on one occasion (median) 1-2 pills, median maximum use: 2-3 pills.
Solowij et al (1992)	Sydney, Australia	N = 100 16 – 48 yrs	Snowball sample of ecstasy users initiated by 12 users known to researchers	On an average occasion, 9% took less than one pill, 71% took one pill, 13% two, 7% more than two. Maximum use on one occasion was reported as 5-9 pills.
Topp et al (1999)	Sidney, Melbourne & Brisbane Australia, 1997	n= 329, 15 -46 years	Snowball sample of current e users (three times in last 12 months) initiated by respondents to newspaper & radio adverts & shop fliers	Average number of pills used on one occasion (median) 1 pill, range 0.5 – 8 pills. Median maximum use: 2 range 0.5-30. 25% had taken 4+ in single episode.16% had injected ecstasy.
Winstock et al (2001)	UK, 1999	n= 1151, no published age	respondents to dance magazine survey, circulation 50 000, rr = 2.3%	Average number of pills used on one occasion (mean) 2.8 pills, 55% took 2 or less, 25% took 4 or more. Maximum reported use on one occasion (mean) 5.8, 54% 5 or more, 5% 10 or more, 2% more than 20. Average number of pills bought (mean) 8.16 (mode 2, median 4), 58% bought 4 or less at a time.

What other drugs are taken by ecstasy users?

Ecstasy users nearly always use other drugs as well as ecstasy. One study reported the average number of substances used by ecstasy users as 3.7 (Siliquini et al 2001), another reported the average number of drugs tried by ecstasy users as 10 (Topp et al). The proportion of ecstasy users who have also used cannabis in their lifetime is reported as 66-100%, used alcohol in their lifetime 95-99.7%, used amphetamines in their lifetime 25-94.2%, used LSD/mushrooms in their lifetime 68-93%, used tranquillisers in their lifetime 27-57%, used cocaine in their lifetime 44-77%, and used heroin in their lifetime 10-32%.

The proportion of ecstasy users who have also taken cannabis at the same time as ecstasy is reported as 79-91%, alcohol with ecstasy 88%, amphetamines with ecstasy 30-83%, cocaine with ecstasy 25-63% and heroin with ecstasy 0-11%. Only one study has specifically looked at what drugs ecstasy users take when coming down from ecstasy (Winstock et al 2001). These were reported as: cannabis 82% of ecstasy users, alcohol 60%, tranquillisers 18%, heroin 2% and cocaine 0.5%.

Table 6: Other substances consumed with ecstasy

Arria et al (2002)	Baltimore – Washington 2000	N= 96, 18 yrs +	Rave attendees leaving 5 nightclubs	Of current users, 95% used alcohol, 81% cannabis, 51% cocaine, 25% amphet, 10% heroin.
Calafat et al (1998)	France, Italy, Netherlands, Portugal & Spain	N= 1 627, 18 – 59 yr olds.	Users & matched controls recruited by snowball	Overall, 36.6% of sample used cocaine with ecstasy, 79.4% used cannabis, 11% used heroin, 35.4% amphetamines
Conner & Sherlock (1998)	UK	N= 164, 18 -38 years	Mailing list of nightclub goers	63% of ecstasy users reported cocaine use whilst using ecstasy
Coulthard et al (2002)	UK, 2000	N= 8 580, 16-74 yrs	Stratified random sample of private households in UK	97% of ecstasy users used cannabis, 77% amphetamines, 63% cocaine, 13% heroin, 27% tranqus, 68% LSD/mushrooms.
Forsyth (1996)	Glasgow UK, 1993-94	N= 135, 14-44 year olds	Snowball sample recruited by drug workers	Of those who used ecstasy, 2.6% reported using cannabis, 11.4% used cocaine, 4.2% alcohol and 12.5% amphetamines at the same time as ecstasy.
Hammersley et al (1999)	Glasgow UK, 1993-1995	N=229, 14-44 years	Snowball sample of 209 ecstasy users + 20 controls	None of these ecstasy users only used ecstasy.
McElrath & McEvoy (2001)	Northern Ireland 1997-1998	N= 50, 17-45yrs.	ads in shops, local music magazine, youth & outreach projects, drug treatment centres, snowballing.	Lifetime prevalence of cannabis use 100%, amphetamines 92%, LSD/mush 86%, cocaine 44%, heroin 10%.
Pedersen & Skrondal (1999)	Norway, 1996	n= 10 812, 14-17 yr olds	total cohort of adolescents enrolled at school in capital city	Of those who had used ecstasy (3%), 65.8% had also used cannabis, 56% amphetamines, 31.5% heroin.
Siliquini et al (2001)	Piedmont, Italy, 1998	n=3274, 18 years	Random sample of military conscripts	Ecstasy users very likely to use ecstasy with other substances, 91% used with cannabis, 61% with inhalants, 54% with cocaine. Average number of substances used if use ecstasy is 3.7
Solowij et al (1992)	Sydney, Australia	N =100 16 – 48 yrs	Snowball sample of e users initiated by 12 e users known to researchers	99% lifetime use cannabis, 83% amphetamines, 84% hallucinogens, 75% amyl nitrate, 77% cocaine, 52% barbiturates, 16% heroin.

Topp et al (1999)	Sidney, Melbourne & Brisbane Australia, 1997	n=329, 15 -46 years	Snowball sample of current users (three times in last 12 months) initiated by respondents to newspaper & radio adverts	Lifetime use of alcohol 99.7%, cannabis 98.8%, amphetamine 94.2%, LSD 93.3%, amyl 75.4%, cocaine 61.4%, BZ 56.8%, heroin 30%, ketamine 18.2%. Mean number drugs tried 10 (2-17).
Tossman et al (2001)	Europe 1998	n=3503, 12 - 49 years	Techno party attendees	Of those who used ecstasy, 30% also took amphetamines with ecstasy, 25% took cocaine with ecstasy.
Winstock et al (2001)	UK, 1999	n=1151, no published age	respondents to dance magazine survey, circulation 50 000, rr = 2.3%	Of those who used ecstasy, at the same time as using ecstasy: 88% also used alcohol, 83% also used amphetamines, 83% also used cannabis, 58% also used cocaine, 51% also used amyl nitrate, 30% also used LSD, 14% also used ketamine. None used heroin at the same time as ecstasy. Used on comedown: cannabis 82%, alcohol 60%, Benzo-diazepines 18%, heroin 2%, cocaine 0.5%.

3 – METHODS

Who is included in this study?

This study is about ecstasy use. People who have not taken ecstasy were not asked to take part in the survey. People who have taken ecstasy we called "ecstasy users". In order to get the largest sample of ecstasy users possible, we decided that anyone who has taken ecstasy before could take part in the study, no matter how long ago. This was so that we did not miss out people who used to take ecstasy but stopped for some reason, as they might have something interesting to tell us, such as why they stopped using ecstasy.

Part of designing a study involving doing research on people is thinking about the effect your research has on them. This is independently reviewed by Research Ethics Committees (REC). All studies have to apply to a REC for ethical approval before the research can start. Our study raised particular problems such as identifying a sample of people who were engaged in illegal activities. We did not include in the study children aged under 16 as the REC felt that we should seek parental consent to involve them in research. As the questionnaire was returned anonymously we could not obtain parental consent.

The sampling strategy was aimed at those living in Devon and Cornwall. People who didn't live in Devon & Cornwall were included in the survey if they were taking ecstasy in Devon or Cornwall at the time of the survey.

We wanted to ensure that there whole of Devon and Cornwall was included in the study. The Steering Committee assisted us with the identification of likely "hotspots" for ecstasy use. The study was frame-worked around 6 geographical centres: Exeter, Barnstaple, Torquay, Plymouth, Newquay and Penzance.

What exactly did we do?

- We asked people to return an anonymous questionnaire about their ecstasy use.
- We asked them to contact us if they were prepared to be interviewed about their ecstasy use.
- We interviewed people about their ecstasy use.

How did we find ecstasy users?

Ecstasy users are a "hidden" population. That is, you cannot look up an official list of ecstasy users as it is an illegal activity and people try to conceal this. However, we know from previous studies that certain people are more likely to take ecstasy than others: those under 35 years of age and those attending night clubs or dance events (see table 4). We wanted to get as wide a range of possible of respondents so we employed four sampling methods:

- A web form that could be accessed by anyone with an internet link. Flyers were designed to advertise the website and the study. These were then distributed by a local distribution company, After Dark Media, to outlets across the South West including all target geographical areas. Outlets included cafes, bars, shops and higher education centres.

- Paper questionnaires with freepost envelopes were distributed outside nightclubs as they closed and at festivals, music and dance events. This distribution was targeted to occur on the Jubilee Bank Holiday weekend when numerous events were scheduled around the South West. It was repeated over a weekend in October when a large dance music event (Godskitchen) was held in Plymouth. After Dark Media distributed the questionnaire inside a "club bag" which included other promotional material targeted at this audience.

- The questionnaire was published in a local events listings magazine, 24/7. This is distributed free at outlets across Devon and Cornwall. People were asked to complete the questionnaire and return it using a free-post address. An editorial about ecstasy use was written for the month the questionnaire appeared.

- People who contacted us to be interviewed were asked if they were interested in assisting with the research. If so, they were asked to distribute questionnaires to other people they knew who took ecstasy. This is known as "snowball sampling", a common method used in drugs research.

What is snowball sampling?

Snowball sampling is a technique commonly used when researching behaviours or conditions that are hidden or in order to reaching a difficult to access population (Bowling 1997). In this case, as taking ecstasy is illegal it is a sensitive subject. People may be happy to discuss this with someone they trust but not with strangers. Snowball sampling uses existing social networks to access hidden populations. For example, ecstasy users we had interviewed were asked if they knew other people who used ecstasy who might be prepared to fill in a questionnaire. If they agreed, we gave them a pack of questionnaires and freepost envelopes. They then gave these to their contacts and asked some of them to pass more questionnaires onto other people they knew. In this way, the number of people sampled "snowballs" from the person beginning the process.

By choosing certain people to initiate snowball samples, particular social groups that are hard to access by the other methods of sampling can be targeted. For example, people who were unlikely to be present at nightclubs such as those aged under 18 years old, the unemployed and the homeless. Questionnaires that were given to each snowball sample initiator were given an ID code so that we could tell from which social network the responses had come from.

What did we do with the responses?

Survey responses were included in a quantitative analysis using descriptive statistics (SPSS v.11) to report about patterns of ecstasy use in Devon and Cornwall. We included demographic data (gender, age, occupation, place of residence) on respondents to get a picture of who they were. We asked them how often they took ecstasy, where they took ecstasy, how many pills they took the last time they used ecstasy and what the maximum number of pills they have ever taken was. We also asked them about other substances they used with ecstasy, when coming down from using ecstasy and at other times.

What did we do at the interviews?

We met people willing to be interviewed in convenient locations that had suitable rooms available for conducting an interview. We explained to them the purpose of the study, what we would be asking them about, gave them a written information sheet and obtained their written consent. Interviews were tape recorded and transcribed verbatim. Any identifying names were removed from the transcripts. Each interview included four main questions that were asked of all those interviewed:

- What was it like the first time you used ecstasy?
- How do you currently use ecstasy?
- What do you think are the risks and benefits of taking ecstasy?
- What other drugs do you use or have you used?

This was so that we could be sure that each of the interviewers (CB and TE) covered similar subjects in the interview. After each of these questions, the interviewers were able to follow up what had been said with any other relevant questions, in order to explore people's opinions and experiences. This method is known as a semi-structured interview with in-depth questioning.

What is a qualitative analysis?

Qualitative analysis describes any analysis that uses non-numerical data (Brown & Lloyd 2001) This is in contrast to statistical analysis which uses numbers to draw conclusions about study data. By using non-numerical data and analysing it qualitatively more detail about the subject of study can be found out. This is useful in looking at subjects on which little research has previously been done. It allows subjects to "emerge" from the data that might not have been thought of before.

How did we do the qualitative analysis?

We used the interview transcripts and the free-text responses on the questionnaires and webforms. We included all of this material in a content analysis (Bowling 1997, Mays & Pope 2000). This means that we read through the data, sorted topics that emerged from what the respondents had said into broad categories that made sense of what they were saying. To assist with this process we used a computer software package designed for qualitative analysis, Atlas Ti (Scientific Software Development, v4.2).

4 - SURVEY RESULTS

Who responded to the survey?

How many people completed the survey?

As of 3rd January 2003, 432 people have returned responses to the survey. Of these, some did not meet the inclusion criteria (21 out of 432, 4.9%) and so were excluded from the analysis of results. Of these, 6 were under the age of 16 years and 15 were illegible. This gives a total of 411 responses included in the results below.

How did they find out about the study?

Just over half of those returning responses used the postal questionnaires handed out as nightclubs closed, and just over a quarter completed the questionnaire through the snowball sample. Just over 10% completed the web form, and just under 10% returned the questionnaire from 24-7 magazine. A detailed breakdown of responses is included in table 7.

People who replied using the different reply methods (i.e. posted form, web form or magazine form) were similar in terms of gender, age, occupation and place of residence.

Table 7: Source of respondents

	n (number of responses)	Percentage
Questionnaire in club bag	218	53.0
Snowball Sample	107	26.0
Web form	52	12.7
Questionnaire in 24/7	35	8.5
Total	411	100

Snowball Samples

Of the twelve people we interviewed, four snowball samples produced returned questionnaires. A further person (non user) started a snowball sample in the North Devon and North Cornwall areas. From these five initiators, 107 responses were returned.

Table 8: Snowball Samples

Location	Occupation	Gender	Age	No. Returned
Redruth	Bar work	Female	23	4
Exeter	NFA / Unemployed	Male	35	55
Exeter	Accountant	Male	34	20
Bude	DJ / Chef	Male	27	13
Okehampton	Stable Manager	Female	30	15

Gender

The gender mix of respondents was roughly equal, with 52.6% stating they were male (216 out of 411), 42.1% stating they were female (173 out of 411) and the remaining 5.4% not indicating their gender (22 out of 411).

Age

The majority of respondents (70.9%) were under 29 years of age. Few were aged over 40 years (31 out of 411, 7.6%). Details of respondents age is summarised in table 9.

Table 9: Age of respondents

Age Group	n	Cumulative percentage
16 - 19	81	20.0
20-24	137	53.7
25-29	70	70.9
30-34	49	83.0
35-39	38	92.4
40+	31	98.8
Total	406	98.8
Missing	5	(1.2)
Total	411	100

Occupation

Nearly two-thirds of respondents were employed (252 out of 411, 61.9%), just under one fifth were students (77 out of 411, 18.9%), a little over one in seven were unemployed (54 out of 411, 13.1%), and a few were homemakers (24 out of 411, 5.8%). A full range of socio-economic backgrounds was covered by respondents, from higher managerial and professional workers to routine occupations and the long term unemployed.

Place of residence by nearest town/city

One third of respondents (33.1%) lived in the Plymouth area and just under one third lived in the Exeter area. The smallest group of respondents lived in the Barnstaple area. A few respondents (4.9%) lived outside Devon & Cornwall. Table 10 details respondents nearest city/town of residence.

Table 10: Place of residence by nearest city/town

	n	Percentage
Plymouth	136	33.1
Exeter	118	28.9
Newquay	52	12.7
Torquay	37	9.1
Penzance	26	6.4
Barnstable	19	4.7
Outside Devon & Cornwall	20	4.9
Total	408	99.3
Missing	3	(0.7)
Total	411	100

Taking Ecstasy

How often did they take ecstasy?

Three-quarters of respondents used ecstasy at least once a month on a regular basis. Table 11 summarises the frequency of use data.

Table 11: Frequency of ecstasy use

Frequency of Use	n	Cumulative percentage
More than weekly	21	5.1
Weekly	99	29.4
Fortnightly	98	53.4
Monthly	87	74.8
Every few months	43	85.3
Occasionally	60	100
Total	408	100
Missing data	3	(.7)
Total	411	100

When did they last take ecstasy?

Over half of respondents had used ecstasy within the last week. 85% of respondents had used ecstasy within the last month. All had used ecstasy within the last 12 months. Table 12 gives the details of respondents most recent ecstasy use.

Table 12: Most recent ecstasy use

Most recent use within...	n	Cumulative percentage
Last week	235	57.2
Last 2 weeks	69	74.0
Last month	43	84.4
Last 2 months	19	89.1
Last 6 months	18	93.4
Last year	27	100
Total	411	100.0

When are they next going to take ecstasy?

Over three-quarters of respondents anticipated using ecstasy within the next month. Some respondents did not intend to use ecstasy again (34 out of 411, 8.3%). Table 13 summarises the data on anticipated next use of ecstasy.

Table 13: Anticipated ecstasy use

Anticipate use within…	n	Cumulative percentage
Next week	150	37.3
Next 2 weeks	88	52.9
Next month	74	77.6
Next 2 months	30	85.1
Next six months	26	91.5
Never	34	100
Total	402	100
Missing	9	(2.2)
Total	411	100

How much ecstasy have they used up till now?

The majority of respondents (320 out of 411, 80.2%) reported using over 50 pills in their lifetime and so may be classified as "heavy" ecstasy users (Reneman et al 2001). This means that the ratio of heavy :: moderate ecstasy users in this sample is 4 :: 1.

Where did they last take ecstasy?

The majority of respondents (40.2%) last used ecstasy in the Plymouth area. Only 4 respondents (1%) last used ecstasy in the Barnstaple area. Over one tenth of respondents last used ecstasy outside Devon and Cornwall. Table 14 details the location of last ecstasy use by nearest city/town.

Table 14: Location of last ecstasy use

Location of last use	n	Percent
Plymouth	165	40.2
Exeter	109	26.6
Outside Devon & Cornwall	61	14.8
Torquay	31	7.5
Newquay	27	6.6
Penzance	13	3.2
Barnstable	4	1.0
Total	404	99.8
Missing	1	(.2)
Total	411	100

In what setting did they take ecstasy?

Respondents reported taking ecstasy in a wide variety of social settings. Whilst 114 reported only taking ecstasy only in a nightclub, 97% took ecstasy in nightclubs, bars, parties or at home. 13% of respondents usually took ecstasy at parties, though few reported parties as the only place they used. Over one third of respondents reported usually taking ecstasy at home, though only 4 reported home as the only place they used. Other places people regularly took ecstasy included on Dartmoor, at the beach, in fields and at festivals. Table 15 summaries the usual setting of ecstasy use.

Table 15: Usual setting of last ecstasy use

Setting of usual ecstasy use	n	Percentage
Night club	329 (114 only place used)	81.2
Party	53 (31 only place used)	13.1
Home	12 (13 only place used)	3.0
Bar	2 (2 only place used)	.5
Other	9	2.3
Total	405	100
Missing	6	(1.5)
Total	411	100

How many pills did they take over 24 hours?

We asked respondents how many pills they took over a 24 hour period the last time they used ecstasy. They reported taking between 1 and 20 pills. Figure 1 shows that the most common (modal) number of pills taken over 24 hours was 2.

Figure 1: Number of ecstasy pills taken over 24 hours on last occasion used

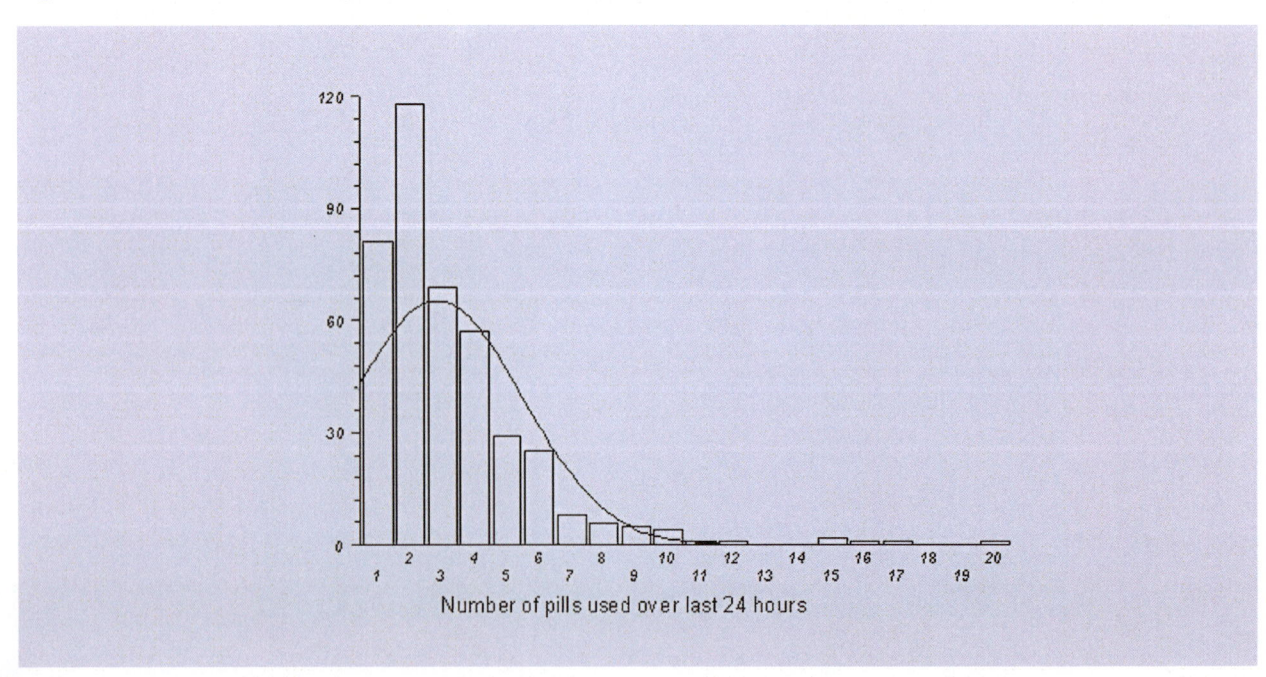

However many respondants took more than two whilst others took fewer. The mid-point number of pills taken (median) was 3. This can be further examined by the use of quartiles and percentiles. From this we can calculate that 25% of people took 2 pills or less, 50% of people took 3 pills or less, 75% of people took 4 pills or less and 90% of people took 6 pills or less. The average number of pills taken (mean) was 3.28, or between 3 and 4 pills.

To explore this further we can look at the graph again. Assuming that the number of pills people take is approximately normally distributed, we can use standard deviation (sd) of the mean to calculate the number of pills people in our sample took over 24 hours the last time they used. Using this method, we can say that 68% of the people in our sample consumed 5.78 pills or less (mean + 1 sd), 95% of people consumed up to 8.28 pills (mean + 2sd) and 99.7% consumed up to 10.78 pills (mean + 3sd).

In case the last time respondents had used ecstasy was unrepresentative we also asked them to estimate their routine use of ecstasy over 24 hours. They said that over an average 24-hour period when they were using ecstasy, they took between 1 and 20 pills. Figure 2 shows the most common (modal) average number of pills taken over 24 hours is 2.

Figure 2: Average number of ecstasy pills taken over 24 hours

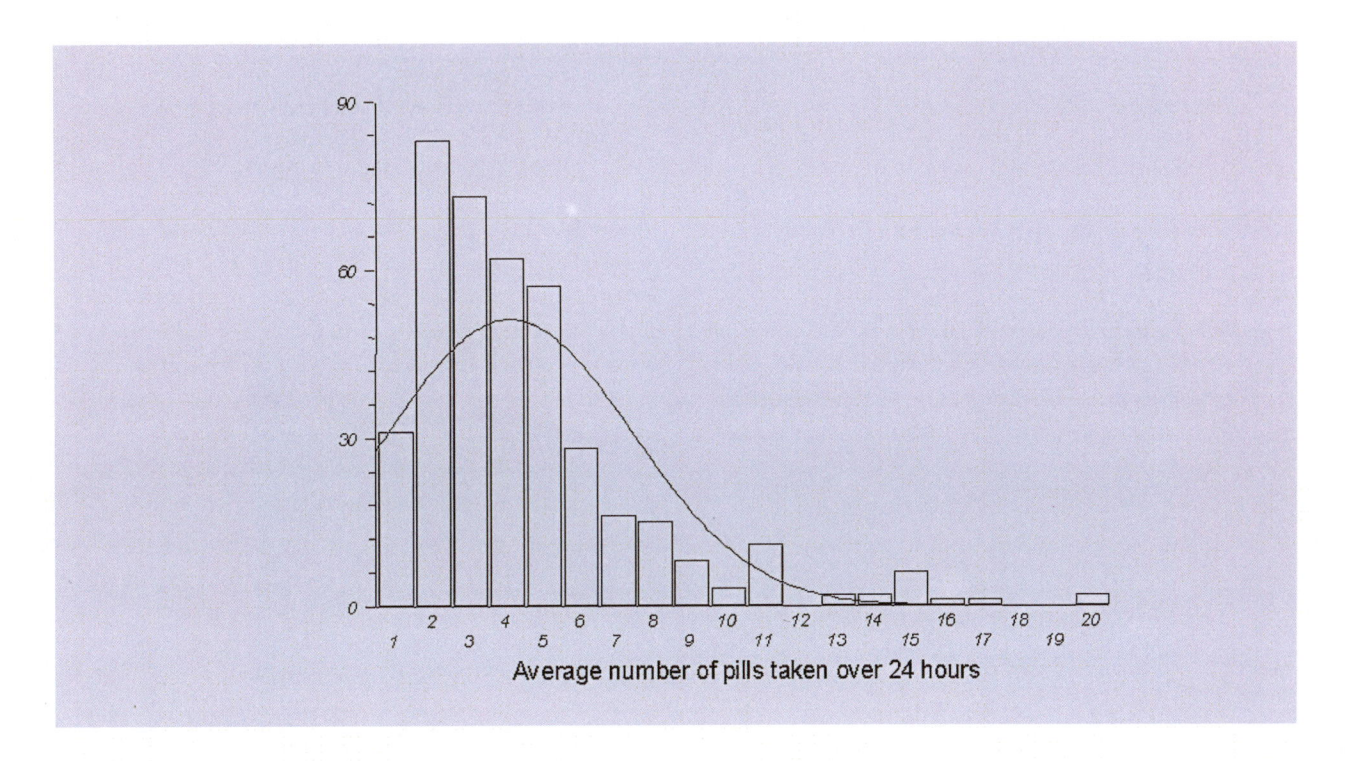

The mid-point number of pills (median) taken over an average 24 hours was four. 25% of people took 2 pills or less, 50% of people took 4 pills or less, 75% of people took 5 pills or less and 90% of people took 8 pills or less. The average number of pills taken (mean) was 4.46 pills, or between 4 and 5 pills over an average 24 hours. Using the standard deviation, we can calculate that 68% of people in our sample used 7.59 pills or less over an average 24 hours, 95% used 10.71 pills or less and 99.7% used 13.84 pills or less.

We also asked respondents about the maximum number of pills they had ever taken in 24 hours. They reported taking between 1 and 35 pills. Figure three shows that the most common (modal) maximum number of pills taken in 24 hours is 4.

The mid-point maximum number of pills taken (median) was seven. 25% of people took 4 pills or less, 50% of people took 7 pills or less, 75% of people took 10 pills or less and 90% of people took 15 pills or less. The average maximum number of pills taken (mean) was 7.91 pills, or between 7 and 8 pills. Using the standard deviation, we can calculate that 68% of people in our sample used a maximum of 13.22 pills or less over 24 hours, 95% used 18.53 pills or less and 99.7% used 23.84 pills or less.

Figure 3: Maximum number of ecstasy pills taken over 24 hours

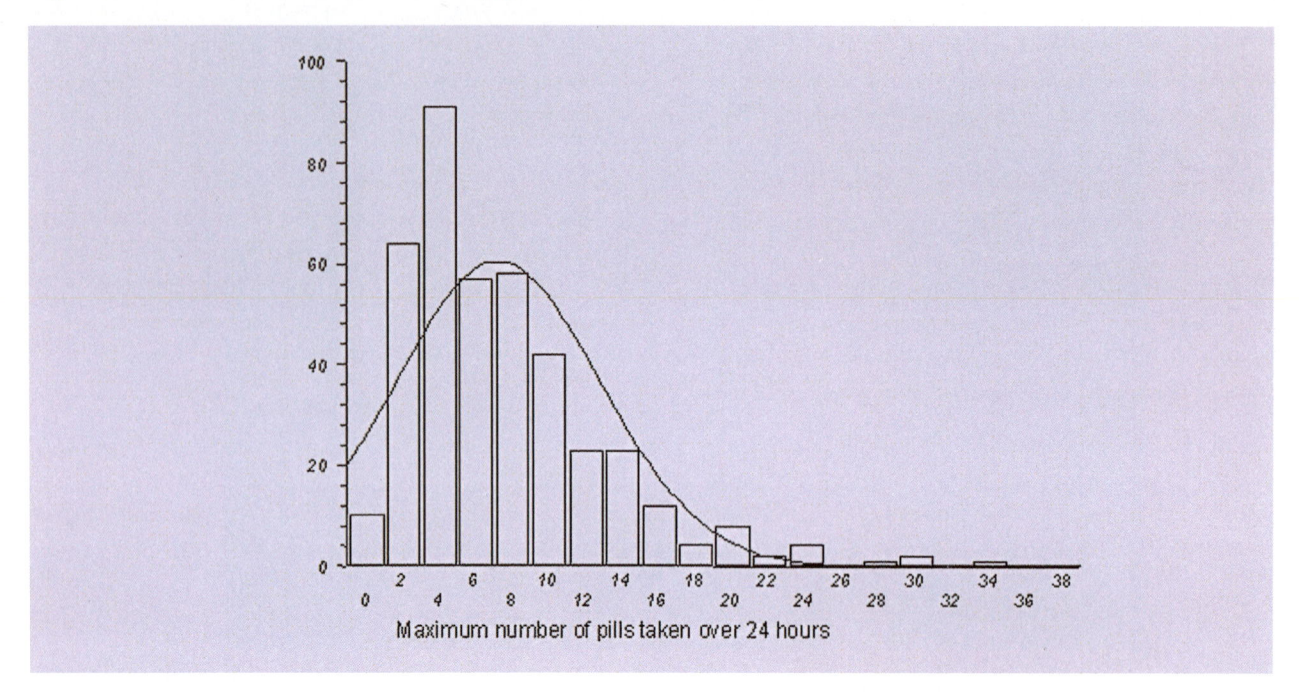

How many pills did they take over a weekend?

We asked respondants how many pills they took over the last weekend they used ecstasy. We told them that the weekend for our purposes ran from Friday midday to Monday midday. They told us that they took between 1 and 40 pills. Figure four shows that the most common (modal) number of pills taken over a weekend is 2.

The mid-point number of pills taken (median) over the last weekend of use was four. 25% of people took 2 pills or less, 50% of people took 4 pills or less, 75% of people took 7 pills or less and 90% of people took 10 pills or less. The average number of pills taken (mean) over the last weekend of use was 5.13 pills, or between 5 and 6 pills. Using the standard deviation, we can calculate that 68% of people in our sample used 9.54 pills or less over the weekend, 95% used 13.95 pills or less and 99.7% used 18.36 pills or less.

Figure 4: Number of ecstasy pills taken over the weekend on last occasion used

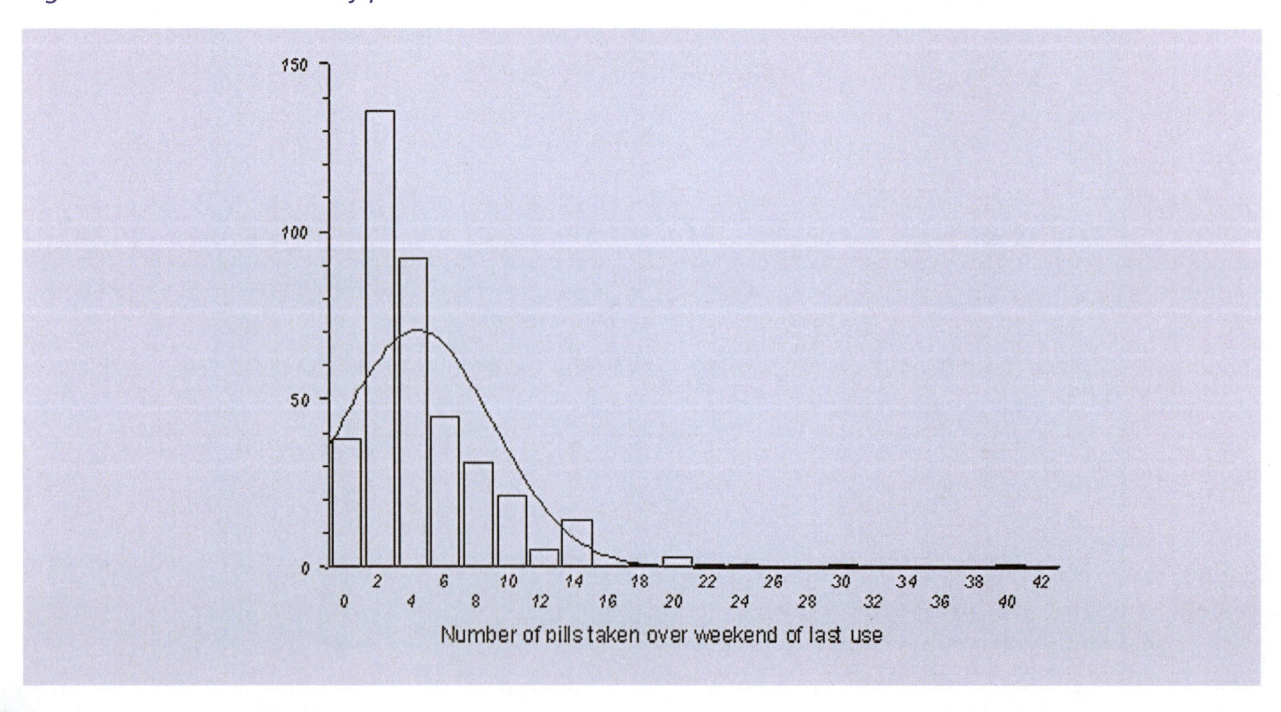

Can we generalise from our sample to the population of ecstasy users in Devon and Cornwall?

Our study sample is a proportion of the total number of ecstasy users in Devon and Cornwall. So our figures estimate of the number of pills used by ecstasy users in Devon and Cornwall. These figures are a "best guess". However, by calculating confidence intervals around the mean values we can say that there is a 95% chance that the true mean lies between two numbers, assuming that our sample is representative.

So we can say that there is a 95% chance that the true mean number of ecstasy pills taken over the last 24 hours of use by all ecstasy users in Devon and Cornwall lies between 3.04 - 3.52. In other words between 3 and 3.5 pills. There is a 95% chance that the true mean number of ecstasy pills taken over an average 24 hours of use by all ecstasy users in Devon and Cornwall lies between 4.20 – 4.88. In other words between 4 and 5 pills. There is a 95% chance that the true mean maximum number of ecstasy pills taken over 24 hours by all ecstasy users in Devon and Cornwall lies between 7.39-8.42. In other words between 7 and 8 pills. There is a 95% chance that the true mean number of ecstasy pills taken over the last weekend of use by all ecstasy users in Devon and Cornwall lies between 4.69-5.57. In other words between 4 and 6 pills.

How many pills did they buy?

There was considerable variation in the number of pills people bought at one time. On average, people bought between 3 and 11. Some people bought a lot more, the most being 500. The details of the average number of pills purchased at one time is given in figure 5.

Were they aware of the risks of taking ecstasy?

Almost all respondents (394 out of 441, 95.9%) reported that they were aware of the risks of taking ecstasy.

Were they confident that the pills contained ecstasy?

Half of respondents (224 out of 411, 58%) reported that they were confident that what they bought and took as ecstasy was in fact ecstasy.

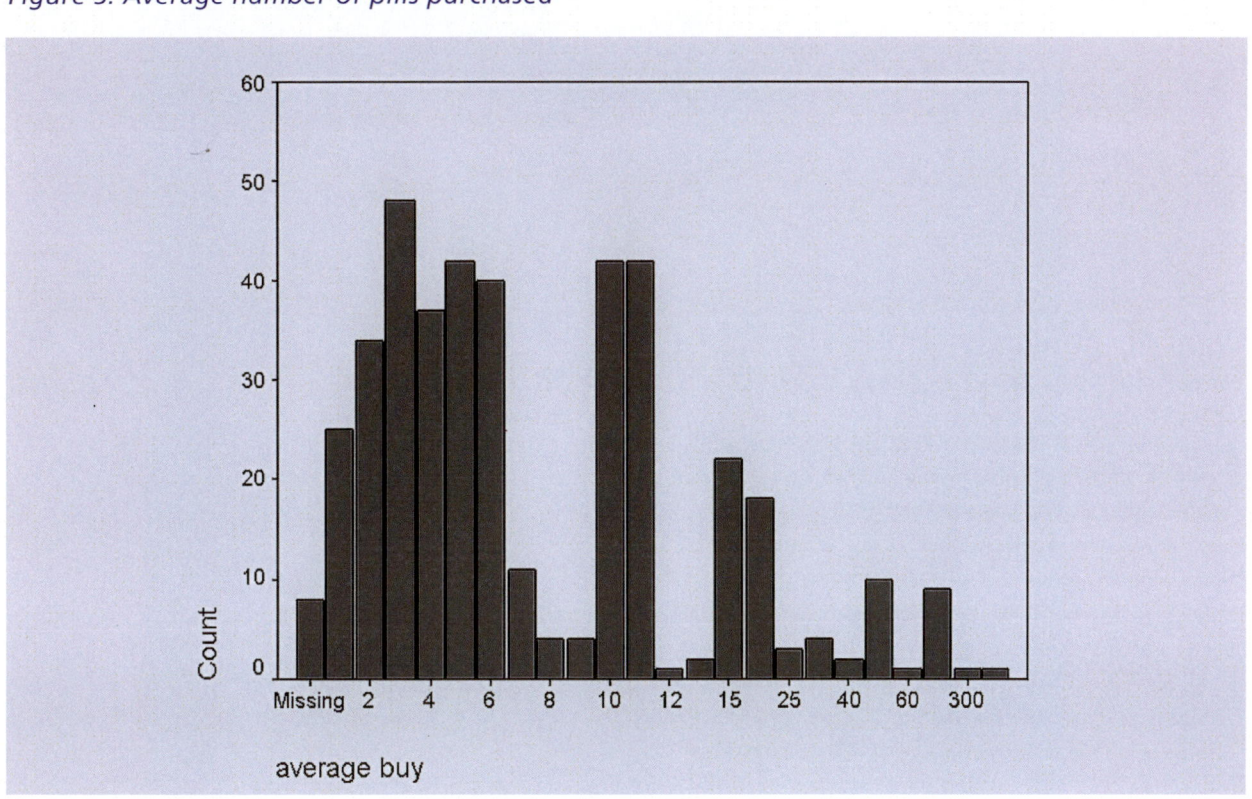

Figure 5: Average number of pills purchased

What other drugs had respondants taken?

What drugs did people use at the same time as ecstasy?

Cannabis and alcohol were the drugs people were most likely to use at the same time as ecstasy, with cannabis slightly ahead of alcohol. Half reported using amphetamines with ecstasy (50.4%) and just under a half of respondents reported using cocaine with ecstasy (48.7%). Thirteen specified that they used crack cocaine. Very few people used only ecstasy (15 out of 411, 3.6%) and nothing else at the same time. Only a fifth of respondents (84 out of 411, 20.4%) used ecstasy with nothing but alcohol and/or cannabis at the same time. Table 16 summarises the data on drugs used at the same time as ecstasy.

Table 16: Drugs used at the same time as ecstasy

	n	Percentage
Cannabis	337	82.0
Alcohol	285	69.3
Amphetamines	207	50.4
Cocaine	200	48.7
Hallucinogens	62	15.1
Sedatives	28	6.8
Crack	27	6.6
Solvents/Inhalers	23	5.6
Nothing but ecstasy	15	3.6
Opiates	13	3.2
2 CB	5	1.2
Poppers	5	1.2
Ketamine	9	2.2

What drugs did people use when coming down from ecstasy?

Cannabis was the drug people were most likely to use when coming down from ecstasy. Less than half of respondents reported using alcohol when coming down from ecstasy. Nearly a fifth of respondents used cocaine after ecstasy use, though very few specified this as crack cocaine. A similar proportion of respondents used either amphetamines or sedatives after ecstasy use. Less than 5% used opiates to come down from ecstasy. Other substances used after taking ecstasy were paracetamol, dioralyte, vitamin C, tea and horlicks. Table 17 summarises the data on drugs used when coming down from ecstasy.

Table 17: Drugs used when coming down from ecstasy

	n	Percentage
Cannabis	335	81.5
Alcohol	219	53.3
Cocaine	79	19.2
Sedatives	65	15.8
Amphetamines	53	12.9
Opiates	19	4.6
Hallucinogens	16	3.9
Solvents/Inhalants	12	2.9
Crack	12	2.9
2 CB	0	0

What drugs did people use when they weren't using ecstasy?

People were most likely to use alcohol and cannabis when they weren't using ecstasy, with alcohol slightly ahead of cannabis. Nearly half of respondents used cocaine when they weren't using ecstasy, though few of these specified that they used crack cocaine. Over one third of respondents also used amphetamines and a fifth used other hallucinogens. Very few people (6 out of 411, 1.5%) used ecstasy and no other substances at all at any time. Less than one fifth of people (76 out of 411, 18.5%) used ecstasy and only alcohol and/or cannabis at any other time. This means that over 80% of ecstasy users in this study took other drugs in addition to ecstasy, alcohol and cannabis. Therefore more than 8 out of 10 ecstasy users responding to this survey were class A poly-substance users. Table 18 summarises the data on drugs used when not using ecstasy.

Table 18: Drugs used when not using ecstasy

	n	Percentage
Alcohol	352	85.6
Cannabis	345	83.9
Cocaine	205	49.9
Amphetamines	171	41.6
Hallucinogens	96	23.4
Sedatives	48	11.7
Crack	34	8.3
Opiates	21	5.1
Solvents/Inhalers	15	3.6
Nothing but ecstasy	6	1.5
Ketamine	6	1.5
2 CB	2	0.5

5 – QUALITATIVE DATA

Data analysis

Interview data

Twelve survey respondents completed interviews about their ecstasy use. Interviewees were selected deliberately to include a wide range of backgrounds and experiences. These ranged from teenage job-seekers to professionals in their thirties. Interviewees lived near Exeter, Plymouth, North Cornwall and North Devon. Demographic details of interviewees are given in table 19.

Survey free-text data

On all survey questionnaires, space was available for free-text responses. Over a third of respondents included free-text comments about their ecstasy use. These were transcribed and included in the qualitative analysis.

Table 19: Demographic data on interviewees

Location	Occupation	Gender	Age
Redruth	Chef	Male	25
Redruth	Bar work	Female	23
Exeter	Unemployed	Male	35
Plymouth	Student	Female	17
Plymouth	Student	Female	27
Exeter	Traveller / Unemployed	Female	34
Exeter	Traveller / Unemployed	Male	37
Exeter	Accountant	Male	34
Exeter	Unemployed	Female	27
Bude	DJ / Chef	Male	27
Plymouth	Job-seeker	Male	18
Plymouth	Student	Male	16

Emerging themes and trends

Both the interview transcripts and the free text data were included in a qualitative content analysis (see Methods section). Five main themes about ecstasy use emerged:

- "Good times"
- "Bad times"
- "E experts"
- "E careers"
- "E v. the rest"

"Good Times"

Respondents spoke about the effects of ecstasy, both immediate and more long-term, what they enjoyed about these effects and what sort of activities they felt were enhanced by taking ecstasy.

Pleasure

Respondents spoke about enjoying the effects of ecstasy:

"The ecstasy rush is the best feeling in the world." Res 96

"I've had some of the best experiences of my life when using ecstasy." Res 167

"Um, to this day, I've had hundreds and hundreds of great times on ecstasy, hundreds." Res G

"Most of the people I socialise with in the context of taking ecstasy are professional people who enjoy a little escapism. After all feeling empathic or 'loved up' towards persons of both sexes in my opinion can't be all that bad." Res 293

"Yeah, yeah, I mean I remember just sitting looking at a soda stream bottle and being fascinated with this glass bottle for about three hours and being loved up with the whole world and all the problems that I'd have didn't seem to matter any more. So it was quite nice." Res D

Long term benefits

Some respondents spoke of continuing beneficial effects they attributed to taking ecstasy over a period of years:

"Been doing a lot of e's most weekends for the past four years. I've noticed no ill effects and remain creative motivated and happy." Res 12

"Since taking ecstasy, I feel that I have calmed down and gained more confidence when using and not using the drug, over varied use for seven to eight years." Res 352

Enhancing music and dancing

Respondents described using ecstasy to enhance music and dancing:

"I use ecstasy is because rave music is my biggest love in life, and ecstasy is the only thing that can make U dance all night and feel good about yourself and the other people around you at the time." Res 96

"with the music going and you get that, sort of, it's like a group buzz, and everyone's like they are all loved up, going: "Wow, yeah, let's dance together" Res E

"Taking pills is not why we go clubbing. It just enhances the experience and our enjoyment of the music." Res 132

"The drug does unlock a creative side in one which is also seen on the dance floor. Many people who prior to taking ecstasy were too afraid to dance for fear of being laughed at can suddenly dance around to the music with creativity and be comfortable." Res 293

Enhancing other activities

They also spoke about using ecstasy to enhance other recreational activities:

"it is normally when you go out clubbing, but, um, the best, I think, the best environment to take it in is sat round with your friends, either after a club or instead of a club. And you just sat round, go for a stomp across the cliffs or whatever and just spend the evening together in a state. I think it is one of the nicest social things." Res J

"You take ecstasy and go for a walk somewhere which is pretty, you know. You've got the energy to do it and all the colours are enhanced. You're not going to get tired. You feel quite smiley, you know, sit there and talk to the squirrels, sort of thing, if you are that way inclined." Res F

"And a lot of people going to the pub, doing pills, people going to football matches doing pills" Res A

"I think now, it doesn't, in my case, and in my friends, certainly my friends case it doesn't have to be the night club, it really doesn't. No. It can be any setting whatsoever and it could be, like, let's all go down on the beach for the day, a couple of cans, just enjoy the sunset, you know. It's quite nice. It doesn't have to be the night time, not no more, although it was evolved around dance" Res G

Developing relationships

Respondents also spoke about using ecstasy to improve and develop personal and group relationships:

"I take ecstasy because it makes me feel more confident to talk to people." Res 96

"the catching of someone's eye producing a smile and being able to hold the glance without feeling uncomfortable" Res 293

"good shagging on it" Res F

"with ecstasy you start to actually discover emotions that you didn't really, you never get to experience them naturally. Like intense euphoria and absolute love is not something you ever get to experience in your daily life. And once you've got there, you can get there again." Res B

"You get to know people a lot deeper than you would if they were just mates from the pub" Res A

"You get the opportunity with Es where when you are in a euphoric state you can actually step back and look at things in a complete different way. For example, say I didn't get on with my mother, at all, but when I was off my head on a pill, I would sit down and I would think about her and I would think: "Well actually, of course, I mean, that's why she's like that, because of this." And, you know, of course she loves me. She's just scared. You see that person for really who they are. So it, from that, you can actually improve yourself anyway, because the next day you are thinking: "God, maybe I'll ring her up and say, 'alright Mum'," like you know, you actually, like, make a bit of an effort. Whereas before, I wouldn't have thought." Res B

"Bad Times"

All interviewees spoke about unpleasant experiences as well as pleasant experiences of ecstasy. These focused on three themes: fear during first use, immediate and long term negative effects.

First Use

Respondents spoke about the fear and anxiety surrounding their first use of ecstasy:

"The leaflets were quite wary and very derogatory about it, and all the press was just horrendous about it, and, um, yeah, it just, it just had a real thing over it to me, it was just like, all I'd heard about it was it was quite unknown and it killed people, so it was just, it was a scare factor. Whereas, all the other drugs, I mean people had been taking for decades." Res J

"Um, yeah, over the time you start to hear about ecstasy and this, that and the other. So I eventually was given it, and, to be honest, I was scared, you know, no-one in their right mind just takes a tablet, you know, so, I, I, the first time I was given ecstasy I, know, for a fact that I didn't do the whole tablet at once, but you know, I wouldn't, I was too scared." Res G

"It was kind of what we thought, so we were quite nervous, so we, well we'll just do a half and see how it goes, which was kind of ridiculous, but that's the sort of mentality." Res K

"well I had a friend, an ex boyfriend whose brother died from taking ecstasy a few years before, so there was that kind of issue." Res D

Immediate negative effects

Respondents spoke about unpleasant effects that they experienced whilst using ecstasy, including paranoia, heat stroke, blurred vision, facial grimacing ("gurning") and feeling uncomfortable:

"I looked across and this person, he could have been totally innocent, looked at the same time and our eyes connected and I started panicking and I swore I was being followed. And in the end I jumped in a taxi and got him to take me back. I even told the taxi driver I said: "someone's following me." It could have been totally innocent. So, like that sort of thing, paranoia, you know, can crack in, yeah, and I'd say that I probably did have quite a few bouts of that." Res G

"we were late getting to the rave and I had two pills and we were late so everything was all hectic and spun out...and I was just freaked and I ended up jumping over the bar and running out the back door and sitting on the beach." Res A

"You'd got lights and it was so hot, and it was really loads of smoke machines, loads of body heat, and it just absolutely overwhelmed me because I was so into it and I thought: "Wow," dancing really full on and flat out, because I didn't know what I was doing. Wasn't drinking enough. And, uh, I missed my midnight counting, because I was sat in St John's Ambulance, just feeling sick and faint, basically, and, uh, they, sort of, sat me down, so just drink some water, slow down, chill out and get some fresh air." Res J

"I've had pills that have had something dodgy in them, which have made your eyes go blurry, to the point that you can't read writing in front of you and stuff." Res J

"you couldn't walk around town on a pill. Just the facial expressions, and you are obviously wasted on it and its quite, I suppose it is quite strong in that way" Res K

"It gave me energy but I had energy anyway, and I didn't really feel loved up, I just felt uncomfortable." Res F

"But what I don't like is that I have no time for anyone else when I'm on E, I find I can be distant and selfish to my girlfriend" Res 141

Coming Down

Respondents also spoke about negative effects after using ecstasy such as low mood and low energy levels s few days after taking ecstasy:

"Tuesdays, the classic Tuesdays syndrome. It seems to be two or three days later, suddenly, you get this real down day, where it really does take it out of you on that one day … you know about two days later you are going to get bad, it doesn't always happen, but, in the summer it was like every Tuesday, you'd see people, and you'd go: "It's Tuesday, yeah," and you'd, sort of, nod at each other and smile and walk on and just, you just a felt a bit, like, sort of, drained and couldn't be asked, and a bit down, I suppose, but nothing too bad." Res J

"Ecstasy needs to be used in moderation otherwise you feel very low emotionally. On Tuesdays or Wednesdays things can be quite tearful" Res 44

"I don't think it was doing my health any good and plus, um, my mental state, perhaps, was becoming really depressed, and I couldn't work out why I was feeling depressed. And I was looking at when I was depressed, it was probably in the middle of the week, after the weekend, or, you know, there'd be things I'd be getting cross about." Res D

"the negative side was, um, the, um, the how spaced out you felt, quite depressed when you come down sometimes. Um, um, how tired your body felt, um, you know, the…all the general come down problems, you know" Res C

"Ecstasy started to give me mood swings + I was depressed for 2-3 days afterwards. Now I've stopped taking it. My nights out are much better and rememberable. I can also do things the next day and eat properly." Res 130

"After the evil comedown from the last session, I think it's high time I gave it up." Res 29

"I stopped due to really bad come downs." Res 142

Negative Long Term Effects

Respondents also spoke about long term negative effects that they attributed to taking ecstasy, including depression, anxiety, paranoia and memory loss:

"I used to use ecstasy a lot more frequently, but I took a long break and now just use it at big club nights. Giving it up completely after a year or so of fairly heavy use was quite strange. I felt very confused for several months and felt like had no direction. I also suffered from mild anxiety attacks, and my state of mind became a lot more susceptible to alteration by the weather – on dull days I just didn't want to do anything – I thought I might have seasonal affective disorder for a while. Friends of mine were hit a lot harder by these effects." Res 18

"I've been using E since 1995, very heavily for 2-3 years, average more than 10+ pills a month. Using a lot less in the last 2 years, due to depressive illness." Res 29

"Used a take a lot of ecstasy but got seriously depressed when had personal problems. I believe the ecstasy changed the chemical balance in my brain. I believe it is a very strong drug." Res 49

"Me + group of friends have all been taking E for over 10 years. Depression is main concern." Res 190

"think it helped trigger my deep long depression. Um, I am sure it did, err, and it's something really I have only just, really only just started to climb out of in the last year, year or two. I noticed, err, it felt to me like, a … a chemical depression rather because everything in my life should have been pointing to me being quite happy. Um, but I wasn't, I was deeply unhappy. Um, and no matter how many times I changed my life, I still seemed, there was this unhappiness, that was new. I hadn't suffered that before. That was a new thing that I'd never experienced before." Res C

"During my time doing ecstasy I found that I became paranoid and kept forgetting things, I strongly advise people to use not abuse." Res 329

"They might not and probably won't kill you but regular heavy use screws up your personality and ruins your quality of life." Res 317

"Haven't done ecstasy for three years abused it quite heavily between 17-19 + brief periods matter of months at a time up until that point. I personally think it has quite severe side effects and noticed on myself and others (brain damage) one pupil bigger than the other. Also I have + others I know have had epileptic fits, dotted over years which we believe to be ecstasy or cannabis related." Res 104

"Nasty stuff! Long term side affect make life quite difficult!" Res 113

"E Experts"

Respondents explained to us their knowledge about ecstasy and discussed how this knowledge informed their decisions about using ecstasy. This included themes on how they weighed up risks and benefits of ecstasy use and how they minimised risk when using ecstasy.

Weighing up the Risks

In weighing up risks and benefits of ecstasy use, respondents compared ecstasy use to other risky behaviours, such as crossing the road. They also compared the risks of ecstasy with those of smoking tobacco and drinking alcohol. They valued being able to choose whether or not to use ecstasy and stated that they accepted responsibility for their choices. The focus was on risk of harm to physical health rather than harm resulting from legal sanctions on ecstasy use.

"Everyone who does & knows the risk involved, but everyone runs a risk when crossing the road but that's not illegal. This isn't small mindedness this is open minded." Res 35

"I'm not saying people don't die from taking illegal drugs, but the number is hugely smaller, but that's the risk when your munching on pills, but when someone puts a cigarette in they're mouth, they will die, when you drink alcohol you rot your liver and then you die, when taking ecstasy you might die, from may be in the pill, its your risk, when its legal, its your choice." Res 295

"There are risks in taking anything. But I don't think that, I think they are pretty negligible, really. I mean they say about the people who died taking it, but, that's not very many really, is it, considering how many people take ecstasy." Res F

"As a knowledgeable professional I know the risks but chose to exercise my right to undertake risky behaviour - I also rock climb and ride motorcycles , driving my car is also potentially very dangerous." Res 294

"Personally I don't give a monkee's if I am caught, I am aware of the risks and feel my 'high' has value to me, as well as being less riskful than cig's and booze." Res 95

"Um, it's too late already, because I have been using it for so long, and it's, I don't use it that often, and there is other things which I do, which are worse, like drinking, I think." Res K

"The professionals (scientists) opinion is always changing and they all have different opinions, I know its damaging me, but its better than alcohol" Res 315

"I don't even think about the risks, if there is one, if there is one, um. Course there's a risk. Um, if you take prescribed medication from the doctors and you get home and the little slip that's folded around the tablets and you open that and it ends up an A4 size if not bigger, then it says: "Possible side effects" If you read them you ain't going to touch that tablet. Let's face it, how many people who, um, get prescribed drugs from their doctor, when they get home, it's a little packet, then they just chuck that away, they don't read that. They get stomach ulcers, infections, bla, bla...oh they are at extreme levels, you know, but you, you would think: "I ain't touching that." With ecstasy you don't get that. You just get the tablet." Res G

"I'm an intelligent person got 1st class degree Social Sciences but work hard and occasional need to let my hair down in combination with an otherwise healthy lifestyle. I feel I have a while to enjoy the benefits of ecstasy use, without totally affecting my long term health." Res 355

"in twenty years if they turn round and say, right, we've now found out this and, you know, I would just kind of say: "Well it's bad luck, I made that choice when I was younger then." But, I don't think that's gonna happen, you know, I'm not afraid of that happening." Res J

"I regard the most dangerous thing about using ecstasy is the fact of it being illegal. I regard this as ridiculous, especially when compared to alcohol" Res 170

Minimising risks

Respondents spoke about minimising personal risk by using ecstasy with others and by being sure that what they took was ecstasy. They were confident that they knew the pills they took contained ecstasy by the look of the pills or their smell, by their price and by buying them from someone that they trusted.

"Although myself and ALL my friends 'do pills' we are aware of the risks, are never on our own and are careful." Res 68

"I am always as sure as I can be that what I buy is E but am aware that it is often mixed with other stuff. I tend to take in halves, so often a cheeky half is enough." Res 7

"Although I have a lot of experience with ecstasy I do not think anyone can be sure what they are buying is MDMA although I could tell if a pill was something completely different." Res 138

"it sounds funny, you open a bag, you open a bag of pills and you smell them, you know straight away if they are good or bad" Res J

"say you get one that's very strong, you can tell when it's a proper pill, you know. It's all crumbly, its very strong. Tasty" Res B

"Well, a lot of them now are clearly marked. You go out and buy, um, something in the high street and 99% of the time they have a stamp on it. And many stamps are quite recognisable, you know, and with me, over the years, I've been buying what I have, you know the main one, you know, so that's one way where I recognise it, or taste. Licking and tasting them" Res G

"I remember I used to pay something like £15 for a tablet, but when you paid that £15 you knew that you were going to have a good night. Whereas now you can pay up to £3- £4, and, you know, it's not the same feeling. It's almost like a speedy feeling, because you're just staying awake, you're not having that feeling that you had five years ago" Res D

"Taking ecstasy for about three years. Always buy from the same people & never had problems." Res 53

"When I say I know what I'm always buying when purchasing ecstasy, I'm as sure as I can be without using testing kit. Plus always the same supplier for all my drugs." Res 63

"I believe if you are knowledgeable and careful you can minimise the risks. Eg testing kit, trusting your dealer, being in full possession of the facts." Res 371

"Usually, I usually buy them off people I know, um, and often they will have tried them before, and otherwise, you don't get…I don't know, you don't tend to buy a lot of dodgy pills from people you know, that's kind of, how it is." Res K

"E Careers"

Respondents spoke about the first time they used ecstasy, how they used ecstasy at the present time and how their use had varied over time. They also discussed what factors affected the amount of ecstasy they used, including discussing whether they felt they had become tolerant to the effects of ecstasy.

Beginning ecstasy use

Respondents spoke about using ecstasy with friends or other more experienced ecstasy users when they first used.

When I first took it was just free festivals really, and during the height of everyone dancing, raving and, um, my friends had taken some and I thought, right, I'll give it a go"
Res E

I think my friend, when we went to the rave, my friend got hold of one off a friend of hers when we were there. And we just did half each. And because it was on you hear all the news about everything, I was really, I was a bit nervous, to be quite honest. It's scary isn't it? Because you don't really know, especially at that age. But, um, as soon as it starts to take effect you realise it's alright really, actually." Res B

"I had been doing, kind of, speed for a little while when I was, it was more of a case at weekends when I had been working quite a lot, and I was really against doing ecstasy because I had heard all the bad press and so I knew that I was quite safe, well, I suppose I could say I was safe taking speed because I knew my limitations. And then the first time was one of my best friends , um, his girlfriend and him was trying it and we were at a house, in their house and, as I said, it was a safe environment, you could try it and you'd be safe." Res D

Everyday use

Respondents reported taking widely different usual amounts of ecstasy. Amounts taken varied considerably for each person at different stages during their life.

"I honestly don't know how many I've done. When I've just had so many on me, you know, but if I went out and done 5, I wouldn't think nothing of that. I wouldn't think nothing of that. I don't think it would be more than 10 in a night, I honestly, I'd be, I'd be surprised at me-self if I'd ever done that." Res G

"it's been, like, quite long periods when I haven't had it every weekend, but, um, last, sort of four weeks, I've been, sort of, just around again but, it's almost like just going out for a drink, or something, it's just part of the, it's part of the make out, but yeah, I suppose it would take, if I was doing it every weekend, you know, on a weekend I would take, sort of, maybe two or three, over a weekend. I mean I do go excessive now, I mean excessive to me now is probably four. Back along, two summers ago, four or five were standard and people were doing eight to ten every night, each, and that's just crazy. But now everyone looks back on it and they all, like, "No way, that was mad." And now they are all, like, sort of, on three, or three or four over a weekend, sort of thing, so it's really calmed down" Res J

"When I was 18, was doing 4 or 5 pills in a night, with other drugs that weekend. It is important to remember that for most of my age, drug taking is a stage we get past" Res 11

"I used to use ecstasy a lot more frequently, but took a long break and now just use at big club nights" Res 16

"Once starting uni I have stopped using ecstasy on a regular basis" Res 374 "my ecstasy use grew from, sort of, say, one or two a weekend, right up to, to the peak time when I was living in Holland one summer, when I was doing them nightly, um, and maybe doing up to, I think I did fourteen one weekend." Res C

High quantity use

Respondents reported several reasons for using more than their usual number of pills. These varied from wanting to maintain a euphoric feeling over a sustained length of time, forgetting how many or how recently they had taken a pill and accidentally using more or using more because of poor quality pills. High quantity use did not produce a greater high according to the number of pills taken, the effects were reported to plateau at a certain level.

"I just think where you take more it's because you're at that height and you just don't want to come down. Although, although one little pill should last you, I can remember years ago, they used to last you all night, just one, like. But now you are looking at a few hours on one, every couple of hours, even though you may not need it, just knock another one, just to boost that. I just think where you take more its because you're at that height and you just don't want to come down" Res G

"Um, on my twenty-fifth birthday it was millennium and I, well, they think, and I think, I am fairly sure I did twenty-four in twenty-four hours. But that was up, awake for, I was awake for thirty-two hours at that point. When people are coming up to you, as well, like that, you know, it's his birthday and, giving you pills right, left and centre, and so on, it's just, it just like, buying yourself, getting bought a drink, you know, it's a constant barrage. It just happened that way, I think, just a build-up. Totally unintentional." Res J

"The quality, yeah. They seem rubbish now. Yeah, yeah. I mean, when I first, the first one I ever did, I think I did pay £15 for. But that kept me going for, sort of, forty hours, you know, and it was lovely, but now, you know, you pay, sort of, £2 for one and you don't even know you've taken it, you know, you [need] four just to realise you've taken a drug." Res C

"the pills now are absolutely crap. I mean they well they are not worth doing. So we get kids that are going out and, well even, like, four years ago, five years ago, you'd go out, and you'd like do two pills in a night and that would be it, because they were good quality, they'd be clean. But now, kids are going out. They're doing between, like, all people we know, they do like between six and ten in the night." Res A

"that's probably why people end up taking more tablets because they're, the high's not the same as what the tablets used to be. It's at different, different level." Res D

"I would say it plateau's off. Yeah, you are just on that level and you just...I would be very surprised if anybody says they go higher and higher. The only time people, I say, use more and more is if they realise they haven't done one an hour ago" Res G

Tolerance

Some respondents spoke about developing tolerance to the ecstasy high with regular use. For some, this led to escalating ecstasy use:

"I realised that this [heavy use] was ridiculous and it had to stop because of the amount I was taking. It was just, you know, you weren't getting the high you were getting when you first" Res D

"I've only been doing E over the last two years. The last one I did may well be the last. The first few times are definitely the best. After a while it actually seems to get in the way but maybe the pills are not as good." Res 392

"I think excessive use is, when you start doing it, like every day, or whatever, or every other day, you do start to feel it and you do start to get, sort of, a bit ratty and you'd sort of need it, like with anything, like smoking all the time or drinking all the time you need that then to keep you going. You get used to it as a crutch." Res J

"It's not the same as it used to be. Don't know if it's the pills or the tolerance you build up. Don't get as much of the loving feeling." Res 59

"suspect that with most drugs, the more you've taken, you, you have a tolerance, even if, I don't know how it is, some drugs are different, but, I mean, I hardly ever take it, but I suspect I've still got that tolerance." Res G

"I think ecstasy you build up a tolerance and you might keep that tolerance and it doesn't fall away that much even if you don't use. Obviously I think it does a bit but not greatly, whereas some drugs like cannabis if you don't smoke for a week and you have a spliff, you, it really does knock you for six. Your tolerance falls away very rapidly but I think your tolerance to ecstasy doesn't." Res C

"I don't, I personally don't think you can become addicted to ecstasy. I think you become addicted to the weekend thing, the whole, you know, friends, the going out, everybody wants and being in love with that crowd, that your, your way of life, don't, I think that's what I became addicted to" Res D

Growing out of it

Respondents spoke about reducing their ecstasy use as they became older:

"They've switched and ecstasy use has dropped right out. I don't know if that's because we are getting older and it's the younger generation now doing it. I think that might be partly the case. But it certainly seems to be a switch with all my age group and, sort of, twenty-four upwards, I suppose, twenty-two upwards. I know it is, like coke and skunk are the main drugs now, and there's a few people doing pills and that, but, I mean, four or five years ago, everyone was doing pills every weekend, and it was huge." Res J

"well the people I know who started off taking it, none of us is taking it any more. Um, yeah, we just don't, it doesn't seem like E. It's not that, that's happened. It's done, it's past, you know. There was like the summer of love, wasn't there, you know, and we were there. We did it. You know, we were up [venue] and all that, you know, and that's in the past. Um, to me, it's just something that, you know, the young generation do now. Um, people my age we, we've done that" Res C

"I think all drugs seem to be something about you grow out of at some point." Res K

"Yeah, well, some of the friends that I still have, or, are used to doing, you know, we used to go out, and I think as we've just got older, we've kind of just realised that it's not all that partying every weekend then." Res D

"E v. the rest"

Respondents compared ecstasy with other drugs.

Ecstasy and alcohol

Respondents spoke about using ecstasy as a safer or cheaper alternative to alcohol or to enhance the effect of alcohol:

"it's kind of a nice thing to use on a weekend because you can usually guarantee that everyone around you is going to be quite chill and loving, whereas if you go out on a piss up, it's always, always ends up in tears or aggro or relationship troubles and it's just like, crazy." Res J

"Ecstasy is cheaper and less expensive than alcohol – about £2 and have a far better effect" Res 114

"I think alcohol is worse than ecstasy" Res 88

"I find alcohol to be the most affective and personality changing drug I have ever done. Alcohol makes me highly aggressive. Ecstasy makes me happy and smiley" Res 102

"the fact that is kills much less people than alcohol, for instance, misses most people" Res C

"I think a lot of people like getting pissed and doing pills because, I don't know, I'm inclined to do it myself because it does, I mean it does calm down the drink but it also, because you've got, the ecstasy is opening you up and making you quite open and quite loving and the alcohol is charging you off and making you quite charged and it's the combination of the two is amazing" Res J

Ecstasy, cocaine and heroin

Respondents made clear distinctions between the use of ecstasy and cocaine or heroin, with heroin being perceived as particularly dangerous:

"I mean I can remember going to parties afterwards and being offered, you know, um, was it rocks? Rocks to come down with and, I just learned that it wasn't a side I wanted to get into. You know, I was quite happy" Res D

If I went out and bought ecstasy and bought cocaine, I would not do ecstasy and then start snorting the cocaine, unless the, if I was definitely sure that the E was literally worn off, you know, then I would start banging on Charlie if I wanted to, but other than that, what is the point?" Res G

"The problem with pills is that the downers' so shit, I moved onto coke instead" Res 77

"I don't think its as dangerous as, um, heroin or crack, um, I think crack is a very nasty drug. But, um, I don't see it as being anywhere in, you know, anywhere near as dangerous" Res C

"Its [ecstasy] not scummy, like you know, brown stuff, for no hopers and Charlie's for people with too much money" Res B

"also because we've used heroin and do know about the pull of that and how, like, I mean, it's got, its almost as if its got its own brain, I swear and it gets in there. I can see what a habit forming drug is and what a habit forming drug isn't . And ecstasy is not habit forming." Res A

6 – DISCUSSION

What are the strengths and limitations of this study?

Was the study sample representative?

As with all research on illicit drugs, it is difficult to know whether the sample of ecstasy users is an accurate reflection of the general population of ecstasy users in Devon and Cornwall. This is because ecstasy users are a hidden population, that is, there is no way of identifying all the ecstasy users from the general population. It is possible that our method of selecting a sample from the hidden population of ecstasy users would introduce bias into the results (selection bias).

Although it is impossible to be absolutely confident that this did not happen as there is no general population of ecstasy users to compare our sample with, we used several means to minimise this source of bias. Also, comparison of our sample characteristics with other published studies on the general population reporting ecstasy use and specific ecstasy user samples show no obvious differences in respondent characteristics (Winstock et al 2001, Sherlock & Conner 1999). Our sample of ecstasy users was selected from known population with high ecstasy use (nightclub questionnaire distribution, events magazine publication) but also recruited from general population targets (webform and flier distribution). We also triangulated sample selection by using purposive snowball sampling to access social groups likely to be missed the previous sampling techniques, i.e. people who do not go to nightclubs, have access to the web or go to dance events. No previous study of ecstasy users has triangulated sample selection to minimise bias in this way.

Because of the ethical issues involved with researching an illegal activity, it is difficult to recruit participants into the study. This has to be done on a voluntary basis as involuntary or covert drug testing is problematic and participants must be confident that their confidentiality will be preserved. This also introduces the possibility of another form of bias, recruitment bias into the study. It may be that people who responded to our survey had particular reasons for making the effort to respond. Again, strategies were employed to minimise recruitment bias by using different recruitment methods, both anonymous postal or webform return and peer-led recruitment by snowball sample. In this way sources of bias were minimised.

In the qualitative study, purposive sampling was explicit and described throughout. Some pre-existing theoretical frameworks were drawn upon for the four standard questions in the interview, that is we thought beforehand about what we wanted to know from the respondents and introduced these questions artificially. This may have restricted the emergence of themes from the data. However, the structured questions were broad and open-ended. Interviewers were then able to follow-up responses with in-depth (unstructured) questioning. Free text responses on questionnaires and webforms were completely open for respondents to express their views.

What new information does this study add?

How many pills do ecstasy users take?

By calculating confidence intervals around the average (mean) number of pills taken we can estimate with 95% confidence the likely average number of pills taken in the general population of ecstasy users in Devon & Cornwall. This gives an average of 3-3.5 ecstasy pills for the last period of use over 24 hours (95% CI: 3.04-3.52), an average of 4-5 ecstasy pills for a routine period of use over 24 hours (95% CI: 4.20-4.88), an average of 7-8 ecstasy pills as a maximum number ever used over 24 hours (95% CI: 7.39-8.42) and an average of 4-6 ecstasy pills for the last period of use over a weekend (95% CI: 4.69-5.57). These calculation are based on the assumption that the study sample is representative of the population of ecstasy users. No previous study has calculated confidence intervals for the average number of ecstasy pills taken over a given time period. Previous studies reporting a comparable range of average and maximum numbers of ecstasy pills taken on one occasion (see table 5).

The qualitative research adds to the information on maximum use of ecstasy pills. Users describe taking pills at regular intervals throughout an episode of use in order to maintain a constant high. There is evidence that the high experienced from taking ecstasy has a plateau effect. High levels of ecstasy consumption (over 10 pills in 24 hours) are reported to be for one of the following reasons:

- As an attempt at sustaining a high over a prolonged period of time, such as a pill an hour for 24 hours;
- As accidental consumption due to forgetting how many or when the last pill was consumed;
- As opportunistic consumption if offered pills.

There is also evidence that the number of pills consumed is related to the quality of the pills consumed, with respondents only needing one or two "good" pills but four or five "crap" pills.

What other drugs do ecstasy users take?

The rate of poly-substance use among this sample of ecstasy users was high, with over 80% taking other drugs in addition to ecstasy alcohol and cannabis. This is consistent with previous studies (see table 6). A high proportion of respondents reported using amphetamine and cocaine at the same time as ecstasy (50% and 49% respectively). This is higher than some previously reported studies (Calafat et al 1998, Forsyth 1996) but slightly lower than one other (Conner and Sherlock 1998). Opiate use on coming down from ecstasy was reported by few respondents (4.6%), though this is again higher than previously reported (Winstock et al 2001). Some authors have argued that the use of opiates on coming down from stimulants such as ecstasy is one gateway into opiate use (Gervin et al 2001). Cocaine use on coming down from ecstasy was reported by nearly one fifth of respondent (19%). This is much higher than previously reported research (Winstock et al 2001, 0.5%). Reported crack cocaine use in this sample was low compared with reported cocaine use (8.3% used crack cocaine at other times from using ecstasy). However, another study (Boys 2002) has reported evidence that many club goers do not realise that cocaine taken in smokeable form is crack cocaine. Further qualitative research would explore this issue further.

An increase in cocaine use over the last year by 16-24 year old has been reported between British Crime Surveys from 1% in 1996 to 3% in 1998 to 5% in 2000 (Ramsey et al 2000). This has led to speculation that "some young people may be turning to cocaine instead of drugs such as ecstasy and amphetamine" (Ramsey et al 2000). In London, the South and Wales, the proportion of 16-24 year olds using cocaine was greater than those using ecstasy (Ramsey et al 2000). In view of the high rate of stimulant use when respondents were not using ecstasy (50% cocaine use and 42% amphetamine use) it may be important to consider this further in Devon and Cornwall. It may be that some of the adverse experiences reported by our sample of ecstasy users were also related to other stimulant use.

Do ecstasy users see their behaviour as risky?

Nearly all respondents believed that they were aware of the risks of taking ecstasy and over half were confident that they knew that the pills they bought contained ecstasy. In the qualitative data, users discussed the risks of ecstasy use in the context of tobacco and alcohol use or of other ordinary behaviours such as car driving. They were clear that taking risks was part of consumer choice. However, the risks of ecstasy discussed by users were focused on the risk of sudden death as reported in the media. This did not take into account other possible harmful effects, such as depression. Users were confident that they could identify good quality ecstasy pills through the pill's physical appearance, the effects experienced once the pill had been consumed and from the reliability of their supplier. Ecstasy users perceived the relationship between themselves and their suppliers as based on trust rather than commercial transaction. It may be that the wider availability of testing kits for street purchased ecstasy pills or publicity of chemical analysis of pill content may confirm or challenge these beliefs.

Is ecstasy linked to depression?

From this study it is impossible to make any causal links between ecstasy consumption and side effects reported. Some respondents did identify low mood 2-3 days after ecstasy use as a usual occurrence but others did not mention this. Others attributed more sustained effects on their mental health to ecstasy use but it is not possible to quantify this from the current study. It may be that those who attributed adverse experiences to their ecstasy use were more likely to respond to the survey. Another study has found evidence that though ecstasy users had higher rates of mental disorder compared with non-users, their first use of ecstasy was after the onset of mental disorder in the majority of cases (Leib et al 2002). Further research would be necessary to examine this hypothesis.

Can users become tolerant to the effects of ecstasy?

One of the surprising themes to emerge from the qualitative data study was that of tolerance to the effects of ecstasy that some users reported. This has not been a focus of previous studies on ecstasy use, though Coulthard et. al. found that ecstasy users were more likely than cannabis, heroin and cocaine users to say that they needed larger amounts of the drug to get an effect (Coulthard et al 2002, p 12). However, reported tolerance to ecstasy may be explained by the unreliable amount and quality of MDMA in street bought pills. This is illustrated out by users comments on the deteriorating quality of ecstasy pills depending on their source. However, it is interesting to note that some users commented that ecstasy pills "weren't as good as they used to be". Further research is necessary to investigate whether this was a result of deteriorating quality or of developing tolerance.

7 – CONCLUSIONS

- Ecstasy users in Devon and Cornwall take an average of 4-5 ecstasy pills over a 24 hour period when using and 4-6 ecstasy pills over a weekend when using.

- The maximum number of ecstasy pills users in Devon and Cornwall have taken over a 24 hour period averages 7-8 pills.

- Whilst taking ecstasy 50% of users have also taken amphetamines and 49% of users have also taken cocaine.

- Whilst coming down from ecstasy 19% reported taking cocaine and 4.6% reported taking opiates.

- When not using ecstasy 50% of users reported using cocaine and 42% of users reported using amphetamines.

- Very few people, 1.5% used only ecstasy and no other substance at any time.

- Over 80% of users took other drugs in addition to ecstasy, alcohol and cannabis.

- Nearly all respondents were confidant they knew the risks of taking ecstasy and over half were confident that what they took was ecstasy.

8 – RECOMMENDATIONS

- In view of the high rate of poly-substance misuse among ecstasy users, drug education interventions on stimulant use, particularly amphetamine and cocaine would enable users to make informed choices.

- Drug testing kits for street bought pills or increased publicity of the chemical analysis of the content of street bought pills may result in a more realistic risk assessment by ecstasy users.

- Further research is needed to investigate stimulant use (including ecstasy, cocaine and amphetamines) in Devon and Cornwall. Links between ecstasy, cocaine and amphetamine use would be of interest in view of their high rate of concurrent use. Of particular interest is the highest ever reported rate of cocaine use (19%) whilst coming down from ecstasy.

- Further research is needed to investigate possible links with depression and ecstasy and tolerance in ecstasy users

REFERENCES

Abraham, M. (1999) Illicit drug use, urbanization, and lifestyle in the Netherlands. Journal of Drug Issues, 29, 565-586.

Adlaf, E. M. and Smart, R. G. (1997) Party subculture or dens of doom? An epidemiological study of rave attendance and drug use patterns among adolescent students. Journal of Psychoactive Drugs, 29, 193-198.

Akram, Gazala and Galt, Myra (1999) A profile of harm-reduction practices and co-use of illicit and licit drugs amongst users of dance drugs. Drugs: Education, Prevention & Policy, 6, 215-225.

Arria, A., Yacoubian, G. S., and Fost, E. (2002) Ecstasy use among club rave attendees. Archieves of Pediatric and Adolescent Medicine 156, 295-296. 2002.

ATLAS.Ti for Windows version 4.2 (1997) Berlin: Scientific Software Development.

Aust, R., Sharp C., Goulden, C. (2002) The Prevalence of Drug Use: Key findings from the 2001/2002 British Crime Survey

Ayer, S., Gmel, G., and Schmid, H. (1997) Ecstasy and Techno - An examination in French-speaking Switzerland. Sucht, 43, 182-190.

Balding, J. (2001) Young People in 2000. Schools Health Education Unit.

Barnard, Marina and Forsyth, Alasdair J. M. (1998) Drug use among schoolchildren in rural Scotland. Addiction Research, 6, 421-434.

Bellis, M. A, Hale, G, Bennett, A,Chaudry, M. Kilfoyle, M. (2000) Ibiza uncovered: changes in substance use and sexual behaviour amongst young people visiting an international nightlife resort. Int Journal of Drug Policy, 11, 235-244.

Boreham, R. & Shaw A. (2001) Smoking, Drinking and Drug use Among Young People in England in 2000. London: The Stationery Office

Botvin, G. J., Griffin, K. W., Diaz, T., et al (2000) Preventing illicit drug use in adolescents: Long-term follow-up data from a randomized control trial of a school population. Addictive Behaviors, 25, 769-774.

Bowling A. (1997) Research Methods in Health. Open University Press

Boys, A., Marsden, J., and Strang, J. (2001) Understanding reasons for drug use amongst young people: A functional perspective. Health Education Research, 16, 457-469.

Boys, A. (2002) Blurred Images: Young cocaine users' perceptions of cocaine. Drug link July/Aug 2002.

Brown, C. S. H., Lloyd, K. (2001) Qualitative methods in psychiatric research. Advances in Psychiatric Treatment, 7: 4, 350-356.

Brown, E. R., Jarvie, D. R., and Simpson, D. (1995) Use of drugs at 'raves'. Scott.Med.J., 40, 168-171.

Calafat, A., Sureda, M. P., and Palmer, A. (1997) Characteristics of ecstasy use in sample of university students and discogoers. Adicciones, 9, 529-555.

Conner, M., Sherlock, K., and Orbell, S. (1998) Psychosocial determinants of ecstasy use in young people in the UK. British Journal of Health Psychology, 3, 295-317.

Corkery, J.M. (2002) Drug Seizure and Offender Statistics, United Kingdom, 2000. Home Office Statistical Bulletin, Research Development Statistics Unit: London.

Cottler, Linda B., Womack, Sharon B., Compton, Wilson M., et al (2001) Ecstasy abuse and dependence among adolescents and young adults: Applicability and reliability of DSM-IV criteria. Human Psychopharmacol.Clin.Exp., 16, 599-606.

Cuomo, Michael J., Dyment, Paul G., and Gammino, Victoria M. (1994) Increasing use of "Ecstasy" (MDMA) and other hallucinogens on a college campus. Journal of American College Health, 42, 271-274.

Coulthard, M., Farrell, M., Singleton, N., Meltzer, H. (2002). Tobacco, Alcohol and Drug Use and Mental Health. London: The Stationery Office.

Dughiero, Giuliana, Schifano, Fabrizio, and Forza, Giovanni (2001) Personality dimensions and psychopathological profile of Ecstasy users. Human Psychopharmacol.Clin.Exp., 16, 635-639.

European Monitoring Centre for Drugs and Drug Addiction, (2002). Annual Report on the State of the Drugs Problem in the European Union and Norway. Luxembourg: Office for Official Publications of the European Communities.

Elliott, Lawrence, Morrison, Anita, Ditton, Jason, et al (1998) Alcohol, drug use and sexual behaviour of young adults on a Mediterranean dance holiday. Addiction Research, 6, 319-340.

Forsyth, A. J. M. and Barnard, M. (1999) Contrasting levels of adolescent drug use between adjacent urban and rural communities in Scotland. Addiction, 94, 1707-1718.

Forsyth, A. J. M., Barnard, M., and McKeganey, N. P. (1997) Musical preference as an indicator of adolescent drug use. Addiction, 92, 1317-1325.

Forsyth, A. J. M. (1996) Places and patterns of drug use in the Scottish dance scene. Addiction, 91, 511-521.

Gerhard, H. (2001) Party-drugs: sociocultural and individual background and risks. Int.J.Clin.Pharmacol.Ther., 39, 362-366.

Gervin, M., Hughes, R., Bamford, L., et al (2001) Heroin smoking by "chasing the dragon" in young opiate users in Ireland: stability and associations with use to "come down" off "Ecstasy". J.Subst.Abuse Treat., 20, 297-300.

Gervin, M., Smith, R., Bamford, L., et al (1998) Chasing the dragon: experience in Ireland and association with "Ecstasy". Addiction, 93, 601-603.

Gold, Mark S. and Tabrah, Haleh (2000) Update on the Ecstasy epidemic. Journal of Addictions Nursing, 12, 3-4.

Gore, S., M. & Drugs Survey Investigators' Consortium (1999). Effective monitoring of young people's use of illegal drugs: meta-analysis of UK trends and recommendations. British Journal of Criminology 39, 575-584.

Grob, Charles S. (2000) Deconstructing Ecstasy: The politics of MDMA research. Addiction Research, 8, 549-588.

Hammersley, Richard, Ditton, Jason, and Main, Donna (1997) Drug use and sources of drug information in a 12-16-year-old school sample. Drugs: Education, Prevention & Policy, 4, 231-241.

Hammersley, Richard, Ditton, Jason, Smith, Iain, et al (1999) Patterns of ecstasy use by drug users. British Journal of Criminology.

Handy, C., Pates, R., and Barrowcliff, A. (1998) Drug use in South Wales: Who uses Ecstasy anyway? Journal of Substance Misuse, Vol 3(2) (pp 82-88), 1998., 82-88.

Hansen, D., Maycock, B., and Lower, T. (2001) 'Weddings, parties, anything...', a qualitative analysis of ecstasy use in Perth, Western Australia. International Journal of Drug Policy, 12, 181-199.

Hendrickson, J. C. (2001) Ecstasy: the key to understanding problem use lies in understanding the users'social networks. Addiction, 96, 1531-1532.

Ho, Elaine, Karimi-Tabesh, Linda, and Koren, Gideon (2001) Characteristics of pregnant women who use Ecstasy (3,4-methylenedioxymethamphetamine). Neurotoxicology Teratology, 23.

Johnston, L.D., O'Malley, P.M., & Bachman, J.G. (2002). The Monitoring the Future national survey results on adolescent drug use: Overview of key findings, 2001, (NIH Publication No. 02-5105). Bethesda, MD: National Institute on Drug Abuse.

Kelley, D. (2001) Rave on. Ecstasy use continues to grow & present new problems for EMS. J.Emerg.Med.Serv., 26, 88-89.

Klee, H. E. (1997) Amphetamine misuse: International perspectives on current trends. Amsterdam: Harwood Academic Publishers.

Klee, Hilary (1998) The love of speed: An analysis of the enduring attraction of amphetamine sulphate for British youth. Journal of Drug Issues, 28, 33-55.

Klitzman, R. L., Pope, H. G., Jr., and Hudson, J. I. (2000) MDMA ("Ecstasy") abuse and high-risk sexual behaviors among 169 gay and bisexual men. Am.J.Psychiatry, 157, 1162-1164.

Korf, D. J., Blanken, P., Nabben, A. L. W. M., et al (1990) The use of ecstasy in the Netherlands. Tijdschrift voor Alcohol, Drugs en Andere Psychotrope Stoffen, 16, 169-175.

Lenton, S., Boys, A., and Norcross, K. (1997) Raves, drugs and experience: Drug use by a sample of people who attend raves in Western Australia. Addiction, 92, 1327-1337.

Manning, Victoria, Best, David, Rawaf, Salman, et al (2001) Drug use in adolescence: The relationship between opportunity, initial use and continuation of use of four illicit drugs in a cohort of 14-16-yr-olds in South London. Drugs: Education, Prevention & Policy, 8, 397-405.

McElrath, K. and McEvoy, K. (2001) Fact, fiction, and function: Mythmaking and the social construction of ecstasy use. Substance Use & Misuse, 36, 1-22.

McElrath, K. and McEvoy, K. (1999) Ecstasy Use in Northern Ireland. 1999. Belfast, TSO Ireland.

McElrath, Karen and McEvoy, Kieran (2001) Heroin as evil: Ecstasy users' perceptions about heroin. Drugs: Education, Prevention & Policy, 8, 177-189.

Meilman, Philip W., Gaylor, Michael S., Turco, John H., et al (1990) Drug use among college undergraduates: Current use and 10-year trends. J.Stud.Alcohol, 51, 389-395.

Miller, P. and Plant, M. (1999) Use and perceived ease of obtaining illicit drugs among teenagers in urban, suburban and rural schools: A UK study. Journal of Substance Use, 4, 24-28.

Millman, Robert B. and Beeder, Ann Bordwine (1994) The new psychedelic culture: LSD, ecstasy, "rave" parties and the Grateful Dead. Psychiatric Annals, 24, 148-150.

Milroy, C. M. (1999) Ten years of 'ecstasy'. J.R.Soc.Med., 92, 68-71.

National House Hold Survey on Drug Abuse in the USA (2001)

Norgaard, L. S., Laursen, M. K., and Lassen, S. (2001) Knowledge, attitudes, behaviour and polydrug use among ecstasy users - A London study. Journal of Social & Administrative Pharmacy, 18, 51-58.

Office for National Statistics (2003) Census 2001: Local Authority Profiles. London: Office for National Statitics.

Pavis, S. and Cunningham-Burley, S. (1999) Male youth street culture: Understanding the context of health-related behaviours. Health Education Research, 14, 583-596.

Pedersen, W. and Skrondal, A. (1999) Ecstasy and new patterns of drug use: A normal population study. Addiction, 94, 1695-1706.

Pope, C., & Mays, N., (Eds) (2000). Qualitative Research in Health Care, 2nd edition. London: BMJ Books.

Pope, H. G., Jr., Ionescu-Pioggia, M., and Pope, K. W. (2001) Drug use and life style among college undergraduates: a 30-year longitudinal study. Am.J.Psychiatry, 158, 1519-1521.

Power, Robert, Power, Tom, and Gibson, Nigel (1996) Attitudes and experience of drug use amongst a group of London teenagers. Drugs: Education, Prevention & Policy, 3, 71-80.

Ramsey, M. Baker, P., Goulden, C., Sharp, C., Sondhi, A. (2001) Home Office Research Study 224.

Reneman L., Booij J., Bruin, K., Reitsma, J.B., Wolff, F. A., Gunning, W.B., Heeten, G. J., Brink, W., (2001) Effects of dose, sex and long –term abstention from use on toxic effects of MDMA (ecstasy) on brain serotonin neurons. Lancet 358, 1864-869.

Riley, S. C. E., James, C., Gregory, D., et al (2001) Patterns of recreational drug use at dance events in Edinburgh, Scotland. Addiction, 96, 1035-1047.

Rome, E. S. (2001) It's a rave new world: Rave culture and illicit drug use in the young. Cleveland Clinic Journal of Medicine, 68, 541-550.

Schifano, F., Oyefeso, A., Webb, L., Pollard, M., Corkery, J., Ghodse, A.H. (2003). Review of deaths related to taking ecstasy, England and Wales, 1997-2000. BMJ 326, 80-81.

Schifano, F., Di Furia, L., Forza, G., et al (1998) MDMA ('ecstasy') consumption in the context of polydrug abuse: A report on 150 patients. Drug & Alcohol Dependence, 52, 85-90.

Schuster, P., Lieb, R., Lamertz, C., et al (1998) Is the use of ecstasy and hallucinogens increasing? Results from a community study. European Addiction Research, 4, 75-82.

Schwartz, R. H. and Miller, N. S. (1997) MDMA (ecstasy) and the rave: a review. Pediatrics, 100, 705-708.

Select Committee on Home Affairs third Report. (2002) The Government's Drug Policy: Is it working? London: The Stationary Office.

Sherlock, K. and Conner, M. (1999) Patterns of ecstasy use amongst club-goers on the UK 'dance scene'. International Journal of Drug Policy, 10, 117-129.

Shulgin, A. and Shuglin, A. (Eds) (1995) PIHKAL: A Chemical Love Story. Berkley, CA: Transform Press.

Siliquini, R., Faggiano, F., Geninatti, S., et al (2001) Patterns of drug use among young men in Piedmont (Italy). Drug Alcohol Depend., 64, 329-335.

Smart, Reginald G. and Ogborne, Alan C. (2000) Drug use and drinking among students in 36 countries. Addictive Behaviors, 25, 455-460.

Solowij, Nadia, Hall, Wayne, and Lee, Nicole (1992) Recreational MDMA use in Sydney: A profile of "ecstasy" users and their experiences with the drug. British Journal of Addiction, 87, 1161-1172.

Spruit, Inge P. (1999) Ecstasy use and policy responses in the Netherlands. Journal of Drug Issues, 29, 653-677.

SPSS for Windows, Rel. 11.0.1. (2001) Chicago: SPSS Inc.

Strote, J., Lee, J. E., and Wechsler, H. (2002) Increasing MDMA use among college students: results of a national survey. J.Adolesc.Health, 30, 64-72.

Topp, L., Hando, J., Dillon, P., et al (1999) Ecstasy use in Australia: Patterns of use and associated harm. Drug & Alcohol Dependence, 55, 105-115.

Topp, Libby, Hando, Julie, and Dillon, Paul (1999) Sexual behaviour of ecstasy users in Sydney, Australia. Culture, Health & Sexuality, 1, 147-160.

Tossmann, H. P. (1997) Ecstasy-pattern, setting and complications of use. Results from an Ecstasy-infoline. Sucht, 43, 121-129.

Tossmann, P., Boldt, S., and Tensil, M.-D. (2001) The use of drugs within the techno party scene in European metropolitan cities. European Addiction Research, 7, 2-23.

Van de Wijngaart, Govert F., Braam, Ruud, de Bruin, Dick, et al (1999) Ecstasy use at large-scale dance events in the Netherlands. Journal of Drug Issues, 29, 679-702.

Van Laar, M. W., Spruit, I. P. (1997) Chasing ecstasy: Use and abuse of amphetamines in the Netherlands. In Amphetamine Misuse: International perspectives on current trends. (ed H. E. Klee), pp. 247-271. Amsterdam.

Van Roon, E. N., Pelders, M. G., and Egberts, A. C. G. (1997) New trends in street drug use. Adam, Eve and their family. Pharmaceutisch Weekblad, 132, 447-452.

Villa, Canal A., Saiz Martinez, P. A., Gonzalez Garcia-Portilla, M. P., et al (1996) Ecstasy users: The search for a psychosocial and psychopathological profile. Anales de Psiquiatria, 12, 183-189.

Webb, E., Ashton C. H., Kelly P., Kamali F. (1996) Alcohol and drug use in UK university students. The Lancet: 348: 922-25.

Weir, E. (2000) Raves: a review of the culture, the drugs and the prevention of harm. CMAJ., 162, 1843-1848.

Wilkinson, S., Myles, J., Soteriou, T., Orme, J., Malinowski, A., Weir, I., Boulton, B., Treagust, J. (2002). The Impact of Drug Misuse on Health in the South West, 1996-2001. Bristol: South West Public Health Observatory.

Williams, H., Dratcu, L., Taylor, R., et al (1998) "Saturday night fever": ecstasy related problems in a London accident and emergency department. J.Accid.Emerg.Med., 15, 322-326.

Winstock, A. R., Griffiths, P., and Stewart, D. (2001) Drugs and the dance music scene: A survey of current drug use patterns among a sample of dance music enthusiasts in the UK. Drug & Alcohol Dependence, 64, 9-17.

Wright S., Klee, H., and Reid, P. (1998) Interviewing illicit drug users: observations from the field. Addiction Research, 6, 517-535.

Wright, J. D. and Pearl, Laurence (2000) Experience and knowledge of young people regarding illicit drug use, 1969-99. BMJ.

Wright, J. D. and Pearl, L. (1995) Knowledge and experience of young people regarding drug misuse, 1969-94. BMJ, 310, 20-24.

APPENDIX A

Steering Committee Membership

Sue Blackford
Force Intelligence Centre
Devon and Cornwall Constabulary

Keith Lloyd
Senior Lecturer in Mental Health
Mental Health Research Group
Peninsula Medical School
Director of R&D
Devon Partnership NHS Trust

Tim Morgan
Teinbridge Drugs Project
Newton Abbot

JJ O'Reiley
Drugs & Alcohol Service Director,
Devon Partnership NHS Trust,
Torquay

APPENDIX B

Survey Form

We would like to invite you to take part in a survey of ecstasy use in Devon and Cornwall. Your participation is entirely voluntary; it is a completely confidential, anonymous questionnaire. You do not have to give your name or any other information that could identify you. Throughout this questionnaire the term ecstasy is used this covers E, MDMA, MDA, MDE, adam, XTC and so on.

What is this survey?
This survey is being done by Christine Brown and Tobit Emmens two researchers at the University of Exeter's Department of Mental Health. Telephone 01392 403421 or email ecstasy@drugsresearch.info. We want to find out how people are currently using ecstasy across Devon and Cornwall. With the information we hope to build a picture of how people are using ecstasy throughout the Southwest.

Who will see my answers?
The information you give is completely confidential and anonymous. We will not know who has responded. The results of the survey will be available on request. We hope that the results will be of use to all those who work with drug users in the Southwest

What are you asking me to do?
Please fill in this questionnaire by ticking the box before the relevant answer or circling the relevant option. Then post it back to us in the envelope provided or use the following freepost address:

DEPARTMENT OF MENTAL HEALTH, UNIVERSITY OF EXETER, FREEPOST (SWB30349), EXETER, EX2 5ZZ

We also want to interview people who use ecstasy about how they feel about ecstasy use, whether they see taking ecstasy as different to taking other types of drugs and what they see as the main risks and benefits of taking ecstasy. A £10 music store token is available to cover travel expenses for interview participants.

If you would be interested in taking part in an interview please call the University of Exeter's Department of Mental Health on 01392 403421 or email: ecstasy@drugsresearch.info You do not have to give your name or personal details.

If you are concerned about your drug use, have any questions or would like more information the following organisations provide free and confidential services

National Drugs Help line
Telephone 0800 77 66 00 (freephone)

Exeter Drugs Project
Telephone 01392 666710

Teignbridge Drugs Project
Telephone 01626 203740/1

Cornwall Community Drugs Team
Telephone 01209 881925

Freshfield Service (Truro)
Telephone 0500 241 952 (freephone)

Harbour Centre (Plymouth)
Telephone 01752 267431

Shrublands (Torquay)
Telephone 01803 291129

Have you ever used ecstasy?   Yes / No

If the answer is No, there is no need to continue as this survey is only about ecstasy use. Thank you for your time. If however, you know someone who does or has used ecstasy, please pass this questionnaire on to them.

A LITTLE INFORMATION ABOUT YOU

Are you: Male / Female

How old are you: ☐ under16 ☐ 16-19 ☐ 20-24 ☐ 25-29
☐ 30-34 ☐ 35-39 ☐ 40+

Are you currently: ☐ Employed ☐ Unemployed
☐ Full-time student ☐ Homemaker.

If employed – please specify

Which ONE of these places is nearest to where you live?
☐ Exeter ☐ Barnstaple ☐ Torquay ☐ Plymouth
☐ Penzance ☐ Newquay ☐ Outside Devon and Cornwall

ABOUT YOUR ECSTASY USE

When did you last use ecstasy?
☐ Last week. Within the last: ☐ 2 weeks ☐ 1 month
☐ 2 months ☐ 6 months ☐ year

Where do you normally use ecstasy?
☐ Exeter ☐ Barnstaple ☐ Torquay ☐ Plymouth ☐ Penzance
☐ Newquay ☐ other town/city

What type of venue? (please circle)
Night Club   Bar   Party   Home   With others   On your own
other – please specify

The last time you took ecstasy how many tablets did you take?

Over a 24h period (please circle)
1 2 3 4 5 6 7 8 9 10 10+   please specify

Over a weekend (a weekend is: midday Friday to midday Monday)
(please circle)   1 2 3 4 5 6 7 8 9 10 10+
please specify

On average, how many tablets might you use in a 24-hour period?
(please circle)   1 2 3 4 5 6 7 8 9 10 11 12 13
14 15 15+   please specify

What is the most number of ecstasy tablets you have ever used in a 24h period?

How many tablets do you estimate you have taken in your lifetime?
☐ less than 50   ☐ more than 50

How often do you use ecstasy? (please circle)
More than weekly   weekly   fortnightly   monthly
every few months   occasionally

On average, how many tablets might you buy in one go?
(please circle)   1 2 3 4 5 6 7 8 9 10 11 12 13
14 15 15+   please specify

When do you next anticipate using ecstasy? (please circle)
Within the next: week   2 weeks   1 month   2 months
6 months   not at all

Do you use any of the following with ecstasy?   Yes / No
If yes, which of the following (please circle)

Alcohol   Amphetamines (Speed)   Cannabis (Dope)

Tranquillisers (e.g. Valium)   Heroin or Opiates (e.g. Methadone)

Hallucinogenics (e.g. acid, LSD)   2CB   Cocaine

Crack (rocks, base)   Solvents/Inhalants

Sedatives (e.g. sleeping pills, downers)   others

Do you use any of the following when coming down from ecstasy?
Yes / No   If yes, which of the following (please circle)

Alcohol   Amphetamines (Speed)   Cannabis (Dope)

Tranquillisers (e.g. Valium)   Heroin or Opiates (e.g. Methadone)

Hallucinogenics (e.g. acid, LSD)   2CB   Cocaine

Crack (rocks, base)   Solvents/Inhalants

Sedatives (e.g. sleeping pills, downers)   others

Do you use any of the following at other times?   Yes / No
If yes, please circle all those that apply

Alcohol   Amphetamines (Speed)   Cannabis (Dope)

Tranquillisers (e.g. Valium)   Heroin or Opiates (e.g. Methadone)

Hallucinogenics (e.g. acid, LSD)   2CB   Cocaine

Crack (rocks, base)   Solvents/Inhalants

Sedatives (e.g. sleeping pills, downers)   others

Are you aware of any risks when taking ecstasy?   Yes / No

When planning to use ecstasy, are you always sure that what you buy and take is ecstasy?   Yes / No

Please add any other comments you wish to make

Thank you for your time. All your answers are confidential and completely anonymous

NOTES

NOTES